WHAT PEOP
PATHW

For many years I have witnessed the Valimont family counsel hurting people who are dealing with prodigals. Thank God there is now a resource to go to and refer to others. This book is a "MUST HAVE" for every follower of Christ!

—Rev. Chad Stafford
Pastor of Coastal Church, Daphne, Alabama

Pathways of a Prodigal is not only a portrait of the prodigal but a mirror for the parents and family of a prodigal. This collaboration of Pastors Randy and Jelly should be in the hands of every pastor and church leader. Don't just go through this book but allow this book to go through you!

—John Kilpatrick, Founder and Lead Pastor,
Church of His Presence, Daphne, Alabama

Over the years I've fielded many questions about my journey as a prodigal, so I'm always on the lookout for a comprehensive and anointed guide for people dealing with prodigals in their home. Frankly, I don't have all the answers, but I know that Jesus Christ, through the blood that He poured out, is THE answer.

Thus, it was great for me to find out about *Pathways of a Prodigal* by Jelly Valimont. It is a tremendous source for the important information and instructions that every believer needs and yet, sometimes embarrassed to ask others about with regard to a wayward son or daughter. This book would have been such a tremendous help for my parents as they were struggling with how to deal with me. I believe this book is valuable and important.

You should read this book voraciously and keep it around when you, or someone you love, are faced with the pitfalls and speed bumps of navigating decisions concerning a prodigal. Jelly Valimont espouses a tremendous prescription that captured my complete attention. *Pathways of a Prodigal* is a must-read for every family!

—Dr. Tim Todd, President & Executive
Director of Revival Fires International

They enter your life with an overwhelming scream that steals your heart like no one else on earth. The dreams and hopes and the love are absolutely elevated for a child. Then the troubled seas of life disrupt, devastate, and destroy what was intended to be the family of a lifetime. Jelly Valimont and her daughter have captured both sides of a prodigal experience and have made sure HOPE is always there because of the promises. If you have ever had a prodigal child, if you have never had a prodigal, if you have ever been a prodigal, this book is a revelation into the journey. . . . tear drop by tear drop, tears of grief, regret, and heartache, and then the tears of reconciliation and the promises in the Word made manifest. I love the raw and the real and this is all of that.

Parents . . . PLEASE read and share this book. It is a source of wisdom, insight, and experience.

—Rev. Maury Davis, President/Executive
Director of Maury Davis Ministries

Pathways of a Prodigal is raw, eye-opening, and extremely confrontational to the average family and parent; however, it will heal and guide the reader through the Holy Spirit to experience healing restoration and lifelong lessons for everyone who reads it.

—Rev. Wayne Blackburn, Senior Pastor,
Victory Church, Lakeland, Florida

I have just completed reading *Pathways of a Prodigal* by Jelly Valimont.... again! I read it once but wanted to go back and read it again. There are books that are written to fulfill a goal of an author and there are books that are written for the life of the reader; *Pathways of a Prodigal* is for the second. I wish that books of this nature did not need to be written, but today it is truly needed.

Jelly Valimont beautifully weaves the life that she and her husband Randy lived with their three daughters. Balancing the home of a pastor's family with a real life. This book takes you on a journey of living life when a child makes the decision to become a prodigal. I feel one of the most powerful statements that Jelly made was, "The prodigal chooses their own way." Too often as parents, we try to find the blame; the blame was a choice. But remembering what she also shared, "Failure is an event, not a person," allows us to move past the choice to wait for the return.

The book will encourage you, challenge you, and inspire you. You will find yourself going back time and again simply to read the "Parents Prayers" at the end of each chapter. I am taking them, using them, and praying them over my own children. As Jelly continued to remind us throughout the book, the prodigal is simply on a journey!

—Dr. Billy Thomas,
Senior Director Church Mobilization Assemblies of God

Copyright © 2024 by Jelly Valimont

Published by Arrows and Stones

All rights reserved. No portion of this book may be reproduced, stored in a retrieval system, or transmitted in any form or by any means—electronic, mechanical, photocopy, recording, scanning, or other—except for brief quotations in critical reviews or articles without prior written permission of the author.

Unless otherwise specified, all Scripture quotations are taken from the Holy Bible, New International Version®, NIV®. Copyright © 1973, 1978, 1984, 2011 by Biblica, Inc.™ Used by permission of Zondervan. All rights reserved worldwide. www.zondervan.com. The "NIV" and "New International Version" are trademarks registered in the United States Patent and Trademark Office by Biblica, Inc.™ | Scripture quotations marked AMP are taken from the Amplified® Bible (AMP), Copyright © 2015 by The Lockman Foundation. Used by permission. www.lockman.org | Scripture quotations marked KJV are taken from the King James Version of the Bible. Public domain.

For foreign and subsidiary rights, contact the author.

Cover design by Sara Young
Cover photo by Valimont Photography/Danielle Bala Photographer

ISBN: 978-1-959095-70-5   1 2 3 4 5 6 7 8 9 10

Printed in the United States of America

Pathways
of a
Prodigal

JELLY
VALIMONT

ARROWS & STONES

To my three daughters: Jordan, Danielle, and Alayna
God blessed your father and me when He gave you to us. You have traveled the life of a "PK," a pastor's kid, with your personal issues but have overcome and been victorious. You have allowed both your father and me to use your lives as examples and illustrations, giving others the understanding that we are not perfect people, not perfect parents, and not perfect children, yet you have risen above circumstances that could have destroyed those not completely grounded in Christ. You have found your hope in Jesus, and for that, I am truly grateful.

To my mother: Olene Jordan
You have been a constant source of encouragement and strength as I have endeavored to complete this book. You have talked me through the days I wanted to quit, the days I decided to give up, and the days I put away the tools of my trade. You told me I could do it when I was sure that I could not. Without you, I am not sure this book would have been completed. Thank you for being there for me.

Contents

Foreword xi

Introduction xiii

Chapter 1. **Parenting 101: The Foundations** 15

Chapter 2. **Identifying the Prodigal** 33

Chapter 3. **Prodigal or Failure?** 51

Chapter 4. **Leaving Home: The Prodigal's Journey** . . . 73

Chapter 5. **The Journey Home** 93

Chapter 6. **The Return** 109

Chapter 7. **Forgiveness and Restoration** 121

Pathways of a Prodigal Notes 137

Foreword

In *Pathways of a Prodigal*, Jelly Valimont embarks on a courageous exploration of one of life's most daunting challenges: the journey of raising a prodigal child. Drawing inspiration from the timeless parable of the prodigal son, Jelly invites us into her world—a world filled with love, loss, and the relentless pursuit of redemption.

As a long-time friend and Jelly's pastor, I witnessed firsthand how Pastor Randy and Jelly exemplified unconditional love and demonstrated total grace and forgiveness.

Through the pages of this book, Jelly shares the raw and unfiltered emotions of parenthood—the joy of watching a child take their first steps, the anguish of seeing them stumble and fall, and the profound hope that guides parents through the darkest of nights.

As you journey alongside Jelly through the trials and tribulations of raising a prodigal child, may you find solace in the shared struggles of parenthood, strength in the face of adversity, and profound joy at witnessing the transformative power of love.

This book ministered to me as a parent as well as a pastor. The principles taught, I can assure you, I will use in my life and ministry to countless other families.

Jelly and Jordan's vulnerability and transparency give us handles as well as hope. Warning: If you pick *Pathways of a Prodigal* up, you will not be able to put it down.

With heartfelt gratitude,
Benny Tate
Senior Pastor of Rock Springs Church
Milner, Georgia

Introduction

Randy Valimont was a phenomenal pastor. This was not his most important role in life. His most important role was that of a husband and a father. In his early years, as with all of us, there was a learning curve. He had to learn to be a great husband and a great father. To do this, he availed himself of the tools at his disposal. He read, studied, and talked to other leaders, husbands, and fathers who had succeeded in their roles in life. He asked questions. He prayed and fasted and sought the wisdom of God.

As our marriage, our children, and our church grew, so did Randy. He continued his joyful journey of being a lifelong learner. As he learned, he also challenged others to do so. One of the questions he frequently asked of people was, "What did you learn from this?" Sometimes the question was asked after a negative experience and sometimes after a great victory. In his opinion, there was always something to learn, something to glean from the experiences of life.

When our oldest daughter became a prodigal, not only were we shocked, but our eyes were also opened to see other parents and pastoral homes who were suffering the same or a similar experience. In true "Randy" fashion, he began to read, study, pray, fast, question, and finally, present tools for others to learn from our experience. The sermon series, "Pathways of a Prodigal," was born from our pain of having a prodigal daughter and learning how to walk through the experience toward victory. We found that our greatest heartache will often produce the greatest tools to help others through their difficulties. As Randy preached the series in our local church and then traveled to share the same message throughout the world, we met devastated parents who found hope in the message.

I do not know how many times the series was reproduced nor how many times it has been viewed through various media outlets. I do know it numbers in the thousands—if not tens of thousands. Randy told pastors to reproduce the series as many times as they wanted. He never wanted remuneration—only for the message to be presented to as many people as needed to hear it. At the end of this book, I have provided a link for the YouTube series, should you want to watch and hear the message as Randy preached it.

This book is born from that sermon series. It is one of the last books Randy indicated to me that he wanted to be written. I hope it ministers to you and gives you hope for your prodigal.

Chapter 1

Parenting 101: The Foundations

There are few things in life as rewarding as becoming a parent. Some are blessed to experience the process of bringing a child into the world, and some are blessed by bringing a child into their hearts and their home. Regardless of how you became a parent, the result is still the same: you are a parent, entrusted with the life and soul of a tiny being. I can remember a friend of mine asking in terror shortly after the birth of her first son, "What if I mess up? How can God really expect me to do this when I can barely take care of myself and my husband?"

Although there are many how-to and what-to-do-if books available now, there are no books that fully unpack the rewards ... or the difficulties! When Randy and I became parents, there were very few parenting books available and the only information we had was what our parents and grandparents modeled. If we wanted to have a godly family, we needed to go to church, teach our children the precepts of the gospel of Jesus Christ, discipline firmly, and enjoy the ride.

Most of the pregnancy and parenting books I read were based on immediate needs. In the doctor's office, I received a very small pamphlet on pregnancy and how to adjust to the demands on my body. In retrospect, I think I needed an entire book on pregnancy! The pamphlet had a whopping two paragraphs on how to take care of a newborn! Ladies in the church gave me valuable advice on pregnancy: how to deal with morning sickness, how to avoid stretch marks, and how to make sure my husband had morning sickness instead of me! After our first child was born, I needed advice on colicky babies, strong-willed children, and how to help my child reach her potential. As more children were born into our family, I looked for resources on birth order, sibling rivalry, and discipline.

Randy and I entered parenthood very trepid but also assured that we could do the job with God's help, our parents' help, and the occasional help and advice from people in our church. God had entrusted to our care this beautiful child, and those who followed our firstborn, as blank slates that we were to fill with God's plans. We dedicated them to the Lord. We rocked all of them a million miles. We prayed before they were born and after they were born. We fasted. We explained. We walked the floors at night. We laughed, and we often failed. Still, we persevered trusting that we were doing the right things. I only dropped one of my children. I only let one roll off the bed. I only let one turn over the shopping cart. Thankfully, it was three different children and no brain damage resulted from the accidents. It seemed that it only took one time for me to learn the lesson! On the other hand,

I think Randy left all our children asleep on the pew after Sunday morning services and came home without them. Thankfully, our home was not that far from the church. None were traumatized or had to go to therapy!

As our daughters grew, we taught them to walk, speak, laugh out loud, sing Sunday School songs and funny songs, say their ABCs, know their numbers, ride bikes both with training wheels and without, ride in wagons without falling out, read and enjoy it, add and subtract, and multiply and divide (and then we let the teachers take over when the math lessons became more complicated.) We taught them to memorize lines for school and church plays, be moral and dress themselves with modesty, keep their speech Christ-like, and welcome into their circle of friends the one whom no one else liked.

We encouraged education and good grades. We offered rewards for making good grades and frequently talked to them about what they wanted to be when they grew up and how to achieve that dream. When the Bible speaks to us about training a child up in the way he should go (Proverbs 22:6), I believe it is speaking of not just training a child in the precepts of following Christ but also training them according to their personality bent. I have seen so many children and their parents become frustrated because, for some reason, the parents think the child should be a math whiz when they are designed by God to be creative, or maybe their strength lies in language and writing.

As young parents, Randy and I tried to give our children opportunities to attempt different activities so they could discover what they enjoyed and where their strengths lie. Piano? Nope. Guitar? Nope. Athletics? Maybe. Sewing? Nope. Crocheting, knitting, tatting? Uhm, maybe? Make-up artistry? Yes. Theater makeup? Yep. Hair styling? Ask my niece, Kristen, and her brother Christopher. Computer coding? Definitely not. Sales? Yep. Graphics? Yes. Ministry? Yep. Vocal performance? Yes, for two of our children, no to the other child. The list goes on and on, but the idea was to give them all the opportunities we could and allow God to show them where they could take those opportunities and use them for Him. It helped to know that they were not just in our hands but FIRST in the hands of our heavenly Father. I don't know that Randy and I ever complained about the money we spent on lessons or instruction that our children eventually decided was not for them. We wanted them to try and experience new things, so we never felt money was wasted.

As parents of teens, our prayer was that if they were ever going to struggle with their commitment to God, they would do it while in our home so we could help guide them. I wish I could say that God answered our prayers that way. He didn't. I am still not sure exactly why He didn't. I do know that it was only after our daughters were on the brink of adulthood that they all struggled with their relationship with God.

Pastors' children see so many good things about the church world, but, unfortunately, they see some of the bad too.

Our children were just like all children who begin to question their belief system once they begin to mature, and it is probably healthy to question what they believe and why they believe it. Preachers' and pastors' kids have so much information about Christian living, theology, and people in the church that it should not surprise us when they begin to question. But it did surprise us. We seemed to think that because they had so much knowledge about the Word and people in general, they should have a better grasp of proper theology! Pastors' children see so many good things about the church world, but, unfortunately, they see some of the bad too. Some pastors and their wives try to hide the bad from their children, but they are not always successful. They see who they believe should be godly people—leaders in the church—verbally attack their parents. They see people get angry and leave the church. They see people who manipulate them to share things they shouldn't. They see people who live one way on Sunday mornings and another way throughout the week.

And these preachers' kids, just like all church kids, begin to question: Why can they do that, and I can't? Why do those people pray for other people when their own lives are a wreck? Why do they say one thing and mean another? Why do they tell lies about me or my parents?

Preachers' and pastors' kids are not exempt from struggling with their relationship with Jesus, and just as they are not exempt from their own personal struggles, neither are their parents. It isn't always a reflection of bad parenting or bad choices on the part of the parents; it could just be the child's bad choice!

I believe that most parents of prodigals will ask the age-old questions of themselves and probably of God, "Where did I go wrong? What did I do that caused my child to walk away from a relationship with Jesus?" There are feelings of condemnation, rejection, and even guilt. The enemy is very good at trying to make us feel all these emotions and questioning us through accusation: "If only you had said," "If only you had done...." Satan will use these feelings of condemnation and guilt to cripple us in our walk with the Lord and leave us feeling like failures as parents and as believers.

There is tremendous heartache and burden in knowing and loving a prodigal, especially if the prodigal is your own child. Before we proceed, allow me to assure you that it is probably not about you. It is more than likely about your child.

Too often, people will look at the parents of the prodigal and blame the parents, not the child. They will question, often to someone else (called gossip), what was going on in that home that would make the child turn away. The parents will feel like failures. They had one (but not really just one) job to do. Just one!—raise this child in the strength and admonition of the Lord. They thought they did, but the child has walked away, and they now feel like failures.

Something that all parents should understand is that a prodigal can come from any home even when a parent has done everything they know to do. You can raise children in the same home, under the same conditions, and somehow, one or more of your children can become a prodigal.

Every person, regardless of how they are raised, who their parents may be, or their life circumstances, must come to a place to understand who God is to them and if they are going to follow Him. Every person must find their own personal walk of faith.

We cannot plan to go to heaven based on the faith of our parents or grandparents. We cannot plan to live with Jesus eternally if we do not come to know Him and decide to live for Him. It has been said many times that God does not have grandchildren. He only has children.

One of the greatest things we can do as godly parents is to lay a correct and firm foundation for our children. The foundation that we lay will one day be the very thing that our children will depend on as they grow into adulthood. The stronger we are and the more precise we are as parents, the fewer questions they will have about our standards and belief systems. I never understood the importance of this in my own life until I became a teenager and heard my friends complain that their parents said one thing at church and in front of their friends but lived another way at home. My parents, who were pastors, strong believers, and disciplinarians, never wavered in their stand for Jesus Christ or in their belief system. If they said it or taught it at church, it was lived out at home. As a result of that, I believe that my sisters and I never questioned the validity of their walk with the Lord.

> **Preventing something from happening is much better than trying to correct it after it has happened.**

Although times have changed, culture has changed, and life has changed, some principles do not change. They remain the same and can lay a firm foundation for you and your family. These principles will help guard against some of the attacks that come against children and cause them to become prodigals. It has been said that an ounce of prevention is worth a pound of cure. Preventing something from happening is much better than trying to correct it after it has happened. On the other hand, these principles are just that: principles. They are a foundation. Basic truths. If you put these into effect in your home, things could still go wrong because your children have free will and must find their own walk of faith as they become adults.

Principles of a Christian Home

Know your own walk with the Lord. Read the Bible. Pray. Be sure your children see you doing these things, not just for show, but as a lifestyle. Pray with them when they get up in the mornings, before you leave the house, before meals, and before bed. Have scripture ready to read or memorize as you head to your daily activities. A chapter or verse in Proverbs is always a good choice. If there is a traumatic event in your life, the first thing they should hear is you calling out to Jesus, not swearing. One of the precious things I remember as a child is hearing my father and mother pray at all hours of the day and night as they interceded for our family and church. Randy followed suit in our home after we married. As a result, our children knew that we had prayer warriors in our family that we could call whenever a need arose. This is a legacy to pass on.

For this reason, since the day we heard about you, we have not stopped praying for you. We continually ask God to fill you with the knowledge of his will through all the wisdom and understanding that the Spirit gives.—Colossians 1:9

Cultivate an atmosphere of peace in your home. We do this in our home by frequently playing praise and worship music. We don't have a television in our living room, so we are not "glued" to programming that promotes confusion. As Matthew 10:13 commands, "If the home is deserving, let your peace rest on it."

Make your major decisions together as a couple and as a family, based on what is best for all, not for only one person. Involve the family in prayer about the decision, asking the Lord for guidance. The first question about a major decision should always be, "Is it God's will?"

But seek first his kingdom and his righteousness, and all these things will be given to you as well.—Matthew 6:33

Find a strong, stable church environment and stay there. Don't move around from church to church, doing the "church hop." Get involved and get your children involved. Sometimes, it becomes necessary to change churches due to various circumstances. If your church is unhealthy, it may be time to make a change for your family.

Prove all things; hold fast that which is good.
—1 Thessalonians 5:21 (KJV)

Prioritize your church attendance. There will always be an excuse to miss. You won't need to look for one. It will easily present itself. Go even if your spouse doesn't go. Prioritize going to church over your children's athletic events. Prioritize church attendance over Saturday night activities. Many churches today offer multiple service times, so you should be able to go! There should never be a question from your children, "Are we going to church on Sunday?" Even if there is sickness in the home, there are opportunities to watch church services online as a family. Believe me, if we ever needed a community of believers to help us in our journey as believers and parents, it is now. We need emotional, physical, spiritual, and prayerful support, as Hebrews 10:24-25 reinforces:

> *And let us consider how we may spur one another on toward love and good deeds, not giving up meeting together, as some are in the habit of doing, but encouraging one another—and all the more as you see the Day approaching.*
>
> *Until I come, devote yourself to the public reading of Scripture, to preaching and to teaching.—1 Timothy 4:13*

Build emotional, spiritual, and physical relationships with your children. Laugh and cry together. Pray and take time to talk about the things of God together. Play together. Work hard and play hard. Life is hard enough without enjoying the time you spend together. Know the personalities of your children and what they enjoy doing. Just like Ephesians 6:4 encourages, do these things with them: "Do not exasperate your children; instead, bring them up in the training and instruction of the Lord."

> *Start children off on the way they should go, and even when they are old, they will not turn from it.—Proverbs 22:6*

Supervise your children; get involved in their school and in their Christian education classes. Be present. A child whose parent is always around is less likely to be mistreated! Know where they are, who they are with, where they are going, and how to get in touch with your children if they are away from you. (GPS trackers on children are not necessarily a bad thing!) Even though a person may seem like a good person, you should KNOW them and watch closely. Invite the friends of your children to your home rather than having your children go elsewhere. We built a pool, so our children's friends would want to come to our house and hang out. I cannot emphasize enough that you need to be involved in the life of your child.

For I have chosen him, so that he will direct his children and his household after him to keep the way of the LORD by doing what is right and just, so that the LORD will bring about for Abraham what he has promised him.—Genesis 18:19

Remember, you are their first line of defense in a wicked world.

Honor the leadership in your church. This applies to pastoral leadership, those in leadership roles, and teachers in the church. When you show proper respect for authority it teaches your children to do the same. You may not always agree with the pastor or the leadership but be extremely cautious about speaking poorly of them. There may come a time when you need spiritual guidance and if you have denigrated the leadership to your children, they will have very little confidence in their prayers or their guidance. Remember 1 Thessalonians 5:12-13:

Now we ask you, brothers and sisters, to acknowledge those who work hard among you, who care for you in the Lord and who admonish you. Hold them in the highest regard in love because of their work. Live in peace with each other.

Don't expect the church to do it all. The church is the support system for what you are supposed to do at home. Talk about the pastor's sermon (in a good way) and what you learned from it, the Christian lessons they included, what was good about the message, and how they took the principles and applied them to their daily lives that week. You can take your children to church every time the doors are open, take them to every activity, and be fully involved. However, if YOU don't follow up with God's principles nor teach them the word of God, it is not enough. Remember, you are their first line of defense in a wicked world.

These commandments that I give you today are to be on your hearts. Impress them on your children. Talk about them when you sit at home and when you walk along the road, when you lie down and when you get up. Tie them as symbols on your hands and bind them on your foreheads. Write them on the doorframes of your houses and on your gates. —Deuteronomy 6:6-9

At some point in time, as they grow, allow your children to begin making decisions about their own convictions and beliefs. This will probably happen as they become teenagers, ready to launch into adulthood. You must trust that you have laid a good foundation for your child to make the right decisions for them. Allow the Holy Spirit to work on them and convict them. He can do a far better job than parents could ever do. Decide in advance what is nonnegotiable in your home. In our home, the nonnegotiable things were called "sin" according to the Word of God. If the Bible said it, we dug in and did not compromise. Another nonnegotiable was church attendance. If you were home, you went. You could go to any service, but you were in church on Sunday morning, somewhere, sometime.

The fear of the LORD is the beginning of wisdom; all who follow his precepts have good understanding. To him belongs eternal praise.—Psalm 111:10

But What About Failure?

Sometimes, you can do all you know to do, lay the correct foundation, and still have a child who fails. One of the things we forget to do as parents is teach our children how to fail. There is a difference between being a prodigal and failing. Too often, we expect our children to grow up following everything we tell them to do, and when they don't do it, we discipline them. I am not stating that discipline or punishment is wrong because it is a fact of life. However, when our discipline is overly harsh or unfounded, we teach them that when they fail, there will be undue pain involved.

I believe in discipline, and I believe that the "punishment should fit the crime." I also believe that if you have never told a child that something is wrong or is incorrect behavior, he or she should not be disciplined for the behavior. Discipline or punishment should be done in private to correct the behavior, restore the relationship, and move forward from the incident. If we continue to go back to the failure and remind the child of what they did wrong, do we not teach them that we expect perfection? Are we teaching them that we won't forget about their failure? Instead, maybe we teach them how to deal with the pain of failure.

How do we do that? What about after the pain? Do we love and embrace them, or do we reject and dismiss them?

Discipline is important for everyone. From the time a child is born, the sin nature wants its own way. That is why a baby cries. The baby is uncomfortable, hungry, or hurting, and he wants someone to make it better. Immediately. Our response is to take care of the problem. Immediately. As the baby grows and becomes a toddler, a preschooler, an elementary-aged child, and finally a teenager, parents must train a child that the world does not revolve around everything the child wants at that moment in time. Yes, we want to help meet their needs, but if they are to learn patience, they must also learn to wait. It is an ongoing process. Discipline must sometimes occur.

When a child is disciplined, he must know that the parent still loves and cares for him, and he must be brought back into the loving embrace of the parent. That helps the child to know that discipline, while painful at the time, will end, and love will follow. However, that should not be the only time that love and care are demonstrated to the child, or the child will begin to misbehave to get what they need: love and care.

In this same way, our heavenly Father cares for us. While we may fail or sin, all we must do is repent, and "he is faithful and just to forgive us of our sins" (1 John 1:9).

So, how do we teach our children to recover from failure? First, and I believe, most importantly, we need to teach them that everyone fails. No one is perfect, and no one is without sin. Secondly, they must learn to admit it as quickly as possible. It is much better to admit it than to be exposed later. Let me give you two extreme examples:

#1: My eight-year-old granddaughter wrote down a word on a piece of paper, so she could remember how to spell it. She didn't look at it during the test, but it was on her desk, which was still potentially wrong. She was caught and, through a process of events, had to admit her failure and take the consequences for her actions. It was much better that she was exposed at eight years old than later in life. She was able to recover from this failure.

#2: During a church service many years ago, the Holy Spirit impressed upon Randy that there was someone who had deep sin in his life who either needed to repent or face being exposed. God told Randy who this was, and Randy went to this man privately to speak to him. The man scoffed, told Randy he wasn't doing anything wrong in his life, and insisted that everything was fine. A short time later, this man's sin was exposed. He lost his business, his family, and everything he owned and spent the next fifteen years in prison. Had he learned to fail and repent, he would not have become the prodigal.

In teaching children to recover from failure, they need to learn how to repent and move forward.

In teaching children to recover from failure, they need to learn how to repent and move forward. Admitting their failure is only half of the equation. If they are to recover, they must repent, say they are sorry, ask for forgiveness, and walk away from their failure. Isn't that just like our own walk with the Lord? Until we admit we are wrong, apologize for our sins, ask for forgiveness, and choose to walk in a different direction from our sinfulness, we are not free. In teaching our children how to fail, we must also admit our own failures—often to them!

The difference between a failure and a prodigal is that a failure may be a temporary event for which forgiveness is offered and received, while a prodigal is one for whom forgiveness is available but not accepted. The prodigal chooses their own way—a life of sinful extravagance, far away from God, sowing seeds that will ultimately reap a painful, sometimes bountiful harvest.

In all of this, remember that Satan hates you. He hates your godly home, your godly children, and your godly spouse. He will do all he can to bring destruction to you and your family. He will find the weakest link in the family and will focus his energies on using him or her to bring about the destruction. Sometimes, that link will be the person with the greatest potential to be used by God. If he can destroy that person, that link that God desires to use greatly could lose their influence on many souls in winning them to Jesus Christ. Knowing and loving the prodigal takes great time and energy, but don't give up. There is great heartache and great burden, but there is still hope. God can still use your prodigal, and we can still call the prodigal home.

You may be at a point in your own life when your children are grown. You may know the principal foundations of a Christian home and realize that you failed to lay it for your home and your children. Maybe your children have walked away, and you are realizing that you may be culpable. What can you do now? Just as we teach our children what to do when they fail, we do the same when we fail. We repent, both to our heavenly Father and to those we have wronged. It is never a bad thing to approach your children and confess that you may have failed them and ask for their forgiveness. Once you have done so, it is up to them to forgive and move forward. Again, we are not perfect parents and while we think we do the best we can with the tools we have, we do make mistakes, and we do fail. However, we must get up from our failures and continue with what God has called us to do.

Your statutes, Lord, stand firm; holiness adorns your house for endless days. —Psalm 93:5

Parent's Prayer

Heavenly Father, thank You for honoring me with the opportunity to raise and imprint this precious child You have given me. I take the responsibility very seriously and hope with all my heart that I can accomplish this great task with which You have entrusted me. Forgive me, Lord, if I have failed to lay a foundation for the principles of a Christian home, and help me to begin again, following Your plan and Your purpose to raise godly and respectful children who will affect Your kingdom. Bring holiness and righteousness into my home. In Jesus's name. Amen.

Chapter 2

Identifying the Prodigal

In Luke 15, we read the age-old story of the prodigal, but we often equate it only with the soul who has departed from a relationship with their heavenly Father. There is another part to the prodigal's story: the one who leaves the home of the Christian parent and godly rearing. Both are heartbreaking, both to our heavenly Father and earthly parents. Sometimes, a prodigal will leave their relationship with God but not leave home. A prodigal only MAY leave home but WILL leave God. That is what makes a prodigal a true prodigal. They turn their backs on God. Once they leave God, there will be a string of broken relationships along the journey.

There isn't much that can rattle the heart of a God-fearing, Christ-following parent like the knowledge that a child they have loved and cared for, trained, and mentored has become a prodigal, often while the child resides in the family home. There may have been signs that the child was headed that way, and while you may have tried to stop the journey, you were unable to do so. Rest assured; you are not alone. God has a prodigal world, so it is within the realms of possibility that we could all, at some point in time, have a child who walks away from everything you have taught them and everything you believe and thought they believed. We can hope and pray that it doesn't happen, but it could. When your child or someone you love walks away from their relationship with God and then walks away from the relationship with you, it can rattle and destroy confidence in your faith and in your ability to believe God for restoration.

> **Pain, trials, difficulty, and heartache all reveal who we really are as the Holy Spirit burns out the impurities in our hearts and in our lives.**

I think we all, at some point in time, will struggle with our relationship with God. We will question who He is to us and whether He truly cares for us. If we want to find the answers and strengthen our relationship with God, we will look for Him and will find Him . . . or He will find us. He may chase us down, but He will never force us to follow Him. The prodigal is the one who has had that relationship or the opportunity for the relationship and has chosen to walk away. By definition, a prodigal is a person who has left home, often under bad circumstances, spends or gives lavishly, and often foolishly. He or she is often extravagantly wasteful and does not consider the future or has a warped view of what could happen in the future.

The questions from the parent are often, "How did this happen? Where did I go wrong? What could I have done differently?"

One thing that we all need to remember is that God sometimes uses pain to accomplish His purpose. Pain, trials, difficulty, and heartache all reveal who we really are as the Holy Spirit burns out the impurities in our hearts and our lives. When we walk through the heartache of having a prodigal, God is not only working in the heart of the prodigal, but He is also working in the heart of the parent to help purify us. He is using pain to accomplish what He needs to do in our hearts. Whatever painful thing we go through in this life, whether in our marriages, with our children, with our extended families, or in our jobs or churches, anything that brings pain should never be wasted. Even when we do not understand, Scripture tells us that God can and will use all things for our good: "And we know that in all things God works for the good of those who love him, who have been called according to his purpose" (Romans 8:28).

Have you ever had an opinion about someone else's issues? Maybe before you had children, you had opinions and ideas about how you would or would not parent your children. Maybe you saw someone make a mistake and decided all the ways their actions were incorrect or how you would have done things differently. Whenever we look at someone else's life and their actions, it is easy to have an opinion, and we can easily become judgmental. It is often when we have personally walked through similar circumstances that we gain understanding and empathy for others' decisions and their actions. Why is that?

God uses our pain and our heartache to produce humility in us and empathy for others.

It is because brokenness creates capacity. When brokenness comes into our lives, regardless of how it comes, it creates a new and deeper capacity for God in us. The brokenness opens our hearts to receive. God uses our pain and our heartache to produce humility in us and empathy for others. You see, brokenness creates capacity, and that capacity should be filled with God's presence and His anointing. Sometimes, we need to come face to face with our limitations, often through brokenness, to see our need for His limitless abilities.

When we are in pain, we become more sensitive. This idea can be applied to physical, emotional, and spiritual pain. Take physical pain as an example. When one has an injury, the last thing you want to do is reinjure the part of your body that is in pain. You guard that part of your body to protect it from pain. You may put a bandage, a brace, or a cast on it. You will do all you can to keep it safe because it is extra sensitive to pain. If someone comes close to accidentally touching the injured part of your body, you almost react before the injured body part is touched.

After years of cheering and stunting, our youngest daughter, Alayna, had shoulder surgery for a torn labrum when she was in college. Her arm was put in a brace to keep her shoulder immobilized. Unfortunately, people misunderstood and thought the injured part of her body was the arm, not the shoulder. They would pat her shoulder and ask what happened to her arm. After a few "pats," we hung a piece of paper on her shoulder that said in both English and Spanish, "DO NOT TOUCH!" Her shoulder was supersensitive to pain due to the surgery. As a result of Alayna's surgery, whenever anyone in the family saw another person with the same type of immobilizer on their arm, we knew not to touch the shoulder. Her sensitivity taught us all a valuable lesson. It created a capacity in all of us to be more sensitive to other's pain because we had seen her experience with pain.

In the same way, the emotional and spiritual pain one endures will create a greater understanding and capacity to be sensitive to what God is trying to say while we face heartache. We listen more closely for the voice of God so that we can hear His instructions and His encouragement. We are more prone to spend time in prayer and Bible reading because we are desperate for a word from God for our situation. Our pain and brokenness have created both capacity and sensitivity. The capacity and sensitivity have created humility and made us more empathetic, more understanding of the pain of others, and more likely to not only hear from God but also help others on their journey through pain and brokenness.

There is an old book titled *Hinds' Feet on High Places* whose main character, Much Afraid, takes the hands of Suffering and Sorrow as she walks through the valley. These are her companions through her trial, never realizing that the Good Shepherd is changing her feet to hinds' feet, so she can traverse the mountains with Him.[1] How similar this is to our lives as we walk with Him through our suffering and sorrow, pain, and heartache, holding His hand and trusting Him to make us more like Him! He is

---
1 Hannah Hurnard, *Hinds' Feet on High Places* (Carol Stream, IL: Tyndale Momentum, 1979).

constantly pushing out the nasty—the fear in us—drawing us to Him and burning out the dross so that one day we will be like the purest gold. Until that day, we learn to hold His hand, painful as it will be, and trust. Just trust.

Children Who Drift

There are no concise answers to why children drift, but there are signs that your child may be headed in the direction of a prodigal.

> **It is much easier to build children than to repair adults.**

One sign is arrogance of the heart. It may not be easily seen. It ranges from a subtle disregard for the rules to blatant crossing of boundaries, disrespect, unwillingness to admit their wrong or their transgressions (even when caught with their hands in the proverbial cookie jar), and deceit. However, just because you may see some of these behaviors in your child does not mean that they are on the prodigal path. It simply means that the potential for a prodigal lifestyle may be brewing, or they are drifting down the wrong path. As parents, it is our responsibility to address the arrogance and bring them to a place of repentance with the help of the Holy Spirit. Often, that can only be done through prayer, especially if the child is already close to their adult years. However, even addressing the issue does not guarantee that the potential prodigal will change their direction. The change in direction only comes from the heart of the prodigal, not parental intervention or discipline.

It is much easier to build children than to repair adults. This is why early intervention, if possible, is best. Our children should know early in life that there is a standard of righteousness in our lives, our homes, and our churches. They should know that if they fail or sin, we will still love and minister Christ to them. They should also know that there are consequences to their actions, to sinfulness. As parents, we cannot always keep them from the consequences of their actions. In doing so, we handicap them, not only as children but as the adults they are to become.

When children begin to drift from the things of God and head toward a prodigal lifestyle, they begin to ignore the laws of God and the rules of the home. In 1 Samuel, we can read the story of the sons of Eli, Hophni, and Phineas: "Eli's sons were scoundrels; they had no regard for the LORD" (1 Samuel 2:12).

The sons of Eli knew the laws of God and pretended to show respect for both, but they never developed a relationship with Him. Sometimes our children know the right things to say and the right ways to act but they never develop a true relationship with Jesus. They follow the rules with their heads and with their will, but their relationship does not become a matter of the heart. Until they submit their heart and their will, they will find it easy to ignore the laws of God and the rules of the home.

The prodigal may pretend to show respect for the ways of the Lord, but given the right opportunity to rebel or make their own decisions about which path they will take, they will not choose the path of Christ.

How many adults do you know who were raised in Christian homes, went to church every time the doors were opened, and were part of boys' or girls' church groups, youth groups, and young adult groups, but somehow lost their way as adults and now want nothing to do with God or church? If you ask them about it, they will often reply that they "tried it but it didn't do anything for them." That may be because they never developed a relationship with Him. They were religious with no intimacy.

Hophni and Phineas, the sons of Eli, were walking away from God but were also driving people away from the Lord with their disrespect for the things of God. As children of the prophet and as priests themselves, they should have been on the journey of drawing people closer to God but were instead driving them away. They were running a "religious racket" by taking the best of the sacrifices for themselves:

> *Now it was the practice of the priests that, whenever any of the people offered a sacrifice, the priest's servant would come with a three-pronged fork in his hand while the meat was being boiled and would plunge the fork into the pan or kettle or caldron or pot. Whatever the fork brought up the priest would take for himself. This is how they treated all the Israelites who came to Shiloh. But even before the fat was burned, the priest's servant would come and say to the person who was sacrificing, "Give the priest some meat to roast; he won't accept boiled meat from you, but only raw."*
>
> *If the person said to him, "Let the fat be burned first, and then take whatever you want," the servant would answer, "No, hand it over now; if you don't, I'll take it by force."*

> *This sin of the young men was very great in the LORD's sight, for they were treating the LORD's offering with contempt.* —1 Samuel 2:13-17

It was only later that their father, Eli, called them to account for their sins. We don't know how long Hophni and Phineas disrespected their father, the ministry, or their role as ministers. Instead, it appears that Eli covered their sins, making them think they were above the need to follow the law. We must instill in our children the need for God and the need to follow Christ.

It is important to note at this point that as we instill in our children the need for God and the need to follow God, there is also a need for holiness. People can pretend to follow God and pretend to love the things of God while living a life of hypocrisy; however, at some time, the sin will be exposed. Our children need to know that hypocrisy is not the accepted norm for God's people. Again, the sooner it is exposed, the greater the opportunity for redemption!

Another sign that children may be drifting into a prodigal lifestyle is they will not only break the rules but will rarely admit their wrong and expect that others will make excuses for them. As parents, we cannot make excuses for our children when they do wrong or break the rules we have put in place. The reality is that when our children do wrong, they should own it. Lying, cheating, stretching the truth, not telling the whole truth, not doing exactly as they are told, and covering for their inadequacies are not helping our children become viable, productive members of society. The reality is that when we "cover" for our children, we teach them that they are above the rules, or the rules do not apply to them. It creates a sense of superiority in them, and this will ultimately lead to arrogance.

There is a time for mercy, but there is also a time for responsibility. If a child is never made to take responsibility for their actions, they will never understand or value an act of mercy. In addition, when a child has committed a wrong or broken trust, parents should give them time to "earn" back their privileges.

My point is this: Trust, once broken, must be rebuilt, not given freely.

For many years, we have had a close relationship with an adolescent drug rehabilitation center for young men. These twelve-to-eighteen-year-old young men live in the residential center for eighteen months. During this time, they receive strong discipleship, are given unbending rules, adhere to strict schedules, and have no contact with anyone other than center staff and family on occasional weekend visits. Some of these young men come to the center by court order, and some come because their families don't know what else to do or feel they have no other options. The longer the young men are in residence, the more privileges they receive. They have the option after eighteen months to stay longer and go into a leadership track so they can also become staff. While the boys are in residence, the parents attend classes and are given tools to help their children succeed as they reenter their homes, family life, and schools at the end of their time in the rehabilitation center.

There have been many young men who excel throughout the program and complete it. They appear to be total winners, rising to the top above all the other residents. Some of these young men have a unique and special touch from God on their lives. They have leadership skills, know the right things to say and do, and all the right things to succeed in the program. They come to church, excel in Bible study, worship the Lord, and have smiles on their faces. When they graduate, if their parents follow the idea of grace and mercy, but WITH responsibility, the boys seem to do well. However, too often we have seen the parents reward the boys immediately after they graduate from the program. They give them cars, cell phones, computers, late curfews, and few boundaries in an attempt to show them how much they trust them. Unfortunately, their attempt to be merciful is mercy, but WITHOUT responsibility. The result is a train wreck. The boys usually return to a rehab center, once again addicted to drugs or alcohol, sometimes living an alternative lifestyle, rebellious, and occasionally in prison. My point is this: Trust, once broken, must be rebuilt, not given freely.

I was recently conversing with someone who told me that he had broken the house rules as a teenager and gotten arrested. When he called home to let his dad know where he was and ask him to bail him out, his father told him that he had a problem. It would be up to him to work it out. The young man could not find anyone to come and get him, so he spent the night in jail. The next morning, his dad arrived to pay his bail and take him home. This man, now an adult and with children of his own, told me he never broke those same rules again.

I was told of another young lady who informed her dad that she was going to get a tattoo, which he had expressly forbidden. She had gone out to eat with her friends and had an appointment after dinner to get her long-awaited tattoo. Her father asked her if she was sure she wanted to do this and go against his rules. She informed him that she was now an adult and could do what she wanted. After they ended the call, her father called the charge card company and canceled her credit card, which was in his name, so she could no longer make charges on the card. Not only could she not charge for her dinner, but she could not charge for her tattoo. When she called back and asked why her charge card was not working, he told her that since she was an adult and could make her own decisions, she could also pay her own way. This was a tough lesson for her to learn, but it was also an important lesson about following the rules of her parents' home.

These last two instances are examples of tough love and holding dependent children accountable for their actions. Too many parents today are making excuses for their children, not standing behind the adults and leaders in the lives of their children, and essentially handicapping their children from becoming strong, godly leaders. What would happen if parents took away privileges from their children when they broke the rules? What would happen if parents stood behind teachers and school officials when their children made poor grades at school rather than telling the children that the teacher was wrong in the way they graded, or the teacher didn't know what they were doing? What would happen if we built respect rather than disdain for authority into our children?

Titus 3:1-2 says this:
> *Remind the people [our children, emphasis on mine] to be subject to rulers and authorities, to be obedient, to be ready to do whatever is good, to slander no one, to be peaceable and considerate, and always to be gentle toward everyone.*

Real repentance is a lifestyle change.

As children begin to drift away from the things of God, they will also begin to devalue repentance. They may even begin to mock repentance: "This sin of the young men was very great in the LORD's sight, for they were treating the LORD's offering with contempt" (1 Samuel 2:17).

Real repentance is not just a momentary experience to make one feel better or to release some of the burden of guilt. Real repentance is a lifestyle change. It is turning and going in a different direction than the one we were previously headed. Even today, we see people who devalue repentance. Salvation cannot happen without real repentance! In our society, pastors and preachers seem to think it is unnecessary to give an altar call or to call people to repentance, often out of fear of embarrassing them. As a result, there is no understanding of repentance. With no public confession of wrong, there is often no humility and no turning from wickedness. When there is a call during a church service for people to come to an altar and pray for repentance, some people will leave, so they don't get stuck in traffic or so they can get to the restaurant first. Some may leave, so they don't feel the conviction of the Holy Spirit and feel the need to repent or change their lifestyle.

I can remember being in church services when the conviction of the Holy Spirit was so strong that people were called out by NAME to come to the altar and repent. I have seen people go to their friends during those same altar calls and implore them to go to the altar and make things right with God. In today's "correctness culture," we are too often afraid of embarrassing someone or hurting their feelings and not concerned enough with calling them into account for sinfulness or questioning their own children about the state of their hearts. Repentance can only come when conviction precedes it. We should be praying for God to convict our children when they sin and give them the grace to repent of their sin.

Whenever someone is convicted of their sin and refuses to repent, their heart has the potential to become hardened to the things of God. When this happens time and again, there may come a time when they will no longer be convicted of their sin. This is how people can sit in a church service with glaring sinfulness in their lives and remain seemingly unaffected by the Word of God, the moving of the Holy Spirit, or the need to repent. The person may even convince themselves that their sin is not really that sinful, they deserve that little bit of sin in their lives, or they will repent later. There can be a myriad of reasons for a lack of repentance. As parents, we should pray for conviction and pray for repentance whenever our children drift away from the things of God or step into sinfulness. I have often prayed for God to convict my wayward children, not allow them to eat or sleep, confuse their thoughts, confuse their relationships, and bring them to repentance. Rarely have I needed to pray that repentance would come, whatever it takes.

Another pathway the prodigal will pursue is immorality. When we think of the term *immorality*, we usually think of sexual sin, but the term is much broader than that. It entails wickedness and sacrilege, things that are subversive and harmful, like murder, lying, stealing, violence, and drug use, and it can also apply to sexual activity outside of marriage and prostitution. When we talk of a prodigal pursuing immorality, it is not just sexual sin. The prodigal may delve into all types of immoral behavior.

In 1 Samuel 2:22-25, we read:

Now Eli, who was very old, heard about everything his sons were doing to all Israel and how they slept with the women who served at the entrance to the tent of meeting. So he said to them, "Why do you do such things? I hear from all the people about these wicked deeds of yours. No, my sons; the report I hear spreading among the LORD's people is not good. If one person sins against another, God may mediate for the offender; but if anyone sins against the LORD, who will intercede for them?" His sons, however, did not listen to their father's rebuke, for it was the LORD's will to put them to death.

The sons of Eli no longer had any shame. We don't know exactly how they had come to that place of shamelessness, why their consciences weren't seared, or why the conviction in their lives was gone. We only know that they had gone so far in their sin that there was no conviction. They were sinning in the temple of God, and there was no correction for their sins. Yes, there was sexual sin, but they were also committing other wicked deeds against God. One of the great sins they committed was not listening to their father when he rebuked them for their sin. Eli should have removed them from ministry and held them accountable for what they were doing. Had he done this, maybe his sons would have understood the gravity of what they had done, and their lives could have been saved. Eli did not administer consequences to them for what they had done.

Consequences are important. When a child understands that breaking a rule will result in discipline or consequences, he or she is less likely to break the rule again. As the child grows and the rules become different, the consequences should be different, but this does not mean that there should be no consequences or discipline. Consequences should still be in place when teenagers and young adults in your home break the rules. Of course, the discipline is vastly different for a young adult than a toddler! As parents, we must decide what rules and standards are important and nonnegotiable in our homes.

One of the first things we convey to our young children is that if we say something, we mean it. If we promise consequences for disobedience, the consequences will occur. When that has been established, there are no questions about IF consequences will follow but WHEN. In the same manner, when our teenagers or young adult children face the promised consequences, it will not be IF but WHEN they will happen. You see, we cannot allow sinfulness to easily reside in our homes, especially if other children follow behind the sinful child and mimic their behavior. Once the standard is set, it must be adhered to with the strength of God and His purpose.

It appears that Eli was a weak parent who raised ungodly sons who mocked and showed disdain for God's kingdom. It is also possible that Eli gave them over to God for God to discipline them for their sin; however, their sin resulted in their deaths. Hophni and Phineas were truly prodigal sons who followed the pathway to destruction.

Parent's Prayer

Heavenly Father, I am in a place of heartache and brokenness today. I am hurting and see that my child may be headed in the wrong direction—away from You and the principles I have tried to teach them. Please help me understand how to help them. Help me to be merciful but also teach repentance with responsibility. I need You to arrest their pathway to destruction. In Jesus's name. Amen.

Chapter 3

Prodigal or Failure?

Failure is an event not a person. Just because you failed doesn't mean you are a failure. It just means you have failed. Get up. Lift up your head. Dust yourself off, pull back your shoulders and keep going.
—John Bosman

As I mentioned in chapter 1, there is a difference between a prodigal and someone who fails. We all fail and have failures to overcome. A prodigal is someone who has failed but has chosen not to return from the failure and instead continues to go further and make wrong, sinful decisions. It is the *lifestyle* of failing that leads to a complete separation from God.

One of the most glaring examples of someone who failed is found in the story of the disciple Peter:

> *Then seizing [Jesus], they led him away and took him into the house of the high priest. Peter followed at a distance. And when some there had kindled a fire in the middle of the courtyard and had sat down together, Peter*

> sat down with them. A servant girl saw him seated there in the firelight. She looked closely at him and said, "This man was with him."
> But he denied it. "Woman, I don't know him," he said.
> A little later someone else saw him and said, "You also are one of them."
> "Man, I am not!" Peter replied.
> About an hour later another asserted, "Certainly this fellow was with him, for he is a Galilean."
> Peter replied, "Man, I don't know what you're talking about!" Just as he was speaking, the rooster crowed. The Lord turned and looked straight at Peter. Then Peter remembered the word the Lord had spoken to him: "Before the rooster crows today, you will disown me three times."
> And he went outside and wept bitterly.—Luke 22:54-62

Peter failed Jesus three different times when he denied that he knew Him. Peter had the opportunity to correct his failure, but he chose not to. He chose to save his own life, to save face, and to walk in his failure and the consequences he set in motion. However, when Peter realized what he had done, he repented. He was sorry for his failure, and he wept over it.

Just as we can make decisions for our children and keep them from making mistakes, God can do the same. However, it teaches others nothing when we make decisions for them. Decision-making is a part of learning and growing in life. God allows us to make decisions, even if they are wrong or sinful ones.

The Bible is full of real people with real problems who made bad decisions. Some turned from God, repented for their failures, and returned to fellowship with God. Some did not repent and return to fellowship with God. Although they are not labeled as such, the ones who did not return to fellowship with God also became prodigals. They spent their lives living lavishly and foolishly.

In 1 Kings 18-19, Elijah had a great victory when he killed the prophets of Baal but became afraid and ran from Jezebel. Here was a man who had won an amazing battle for the Lord but ran from a wicked woman and failed for a moment. He forgot to trust God quickly after a victory, but God did not turn His back on Elijah. God treated him with compassion, food, and rest. After a time, Elijah was refreshed and renewed, and God again chose to use him. Elijah may have failed but went back the way he came, and he finished strong!

Adam and Eve failed God but returned to fellowship with Him (Genesis 3).

Abraham and Sarah failed God, but God still used them to make a mighty nation (Genesis 16).

Samson was a Nazarite who was set aside for God, yet he failed. He became enamored with Delilah, and through her manipulation, he failed God and his people and lost the strength the Lord had given him. However, after his failure, Samson asked God to remember him. God restored his strength, and he was able to kill more Philistines when he died than before his failure (Judges 16).

There were entire nations who turned from God in failure and faced dire consequences. Both Sodom and Gomorrah were destroyed due to their wickedness (Genesis 19).

In chapter one of this book, I briefly touched on failure and teaching our children to fail as part of our parenting plan. If we teach our children what to do when they fail, they will be more equipped to rise from their failures. However, there are times when we do not immediately rise from the failures in our lives.

If no one ever failed, we would all be perfect people, but we are not. No one escapes failure. We all have sin, and we all have failures. It is up to us as to how we deal with the failures and the sin in our lives and how or if we move forward in grace. Failure may be small, or it may be large, glaring, and public. Either way, we should learn from it so we don't have to repeat it!

There are some important things we need to understand about failure, things that we should know for our own lives and then convey to our children as they navigate their failures.

Failure is not final unless we allow it to be final.

First, failure is not final unless we allow it to be final. We have all known people who failed. We all know someone who has admitted their failure, repented, and moved forward into restoration. Likewise, we all know someone who has failed and chosen not to repent and seek restoration. I could give you examples of broken homes and broken lives, of men and women who fell into sinfulness and, from all appearances, died in their sin. The good news is that if the thief on the cross asked Jesus to remember him when he came into his kingdom, and Jesus assured him that he would, we can also hold on to the hope that those who have failed and entered eternity may have taken the last fleeting moments of their lives to repent for their sins. I am not God, and I do not make those decisions, but I do serve a God who is full of grace and kindness and knows the hearts of men. There is always hope.

Second, failure can produce brokenness, and broken things can be beautiful. God sees who we will become. He doesn't just see all our faults and failures. He sees the finished product.

When we fail, God still offers forgiveness. He doesn't want us to fail, but mercy is still available.

I believe that one of the reasons Satan attacks and goes after certain children in families is because there is a great destiny in their lives. Just as we may sense someone who has a call of God on their lives, Satan also understands this. As ministers and leaders, I can tell you that there are young people who will demonstrate that they are going to make it in ministry and others who will demonstrate that they are not. Sometimes, that is because they take shortcuts, do all they can to avoid responsibility, or may have no work ethic or spiritual passion. Some may fall into sinfulness unintentionally, but others may predetermine that they are going to do their own thing and go their own way just because they want to. They predetermine that they are going to walk boldly into a life of sinfulness.

When we were in college, certain people seemed to have a special call on their lives. They were the cream of the crop, so to speak. Everyone wanted to be them or be around them. Even at a young age, they preached revivals, were called on to speak in chapel services, and traveled and represented the college. The administration loved them! However, we, as students, saw them and heard their conversations during the week. We knew their immorality. We knew how they cheated during exam time. We knew the anointed sermons they preached were not their own work but taken from someone else. We knew their dishonesty. It seemed as if there were no consequences for their actions. They were the ones taking shortcuts, avoiding responsibility, and doing what they wanted to do because they could. They were not truly serving Jesus; it only seemed they were. They had decided that they could do what they wanted to do, even in ministry, and it would be okay. It wasn't long after we graduated that we learned these prodigal ministers, one after another, were facing massive failures in their lives and would be required to live in the pigpen they made for themselves. Their sin was premeditated and predetermined, and although they had a strong call on their lives, they needed to find a way back from failure into repentance and restoration. I would love to tell you that all of them did. Unfortunately, some did, and some did not.

Our personal note: I will not tell you that as parents or pastors that we did everything correctly, but I will tell you that we did the best we could with the tools we had. We prayed, we committed our children to God, and we tried to lead our church families in the same ways. It was hard.

We began building a new sanctuary in 2001, just before the 9/11 attacks on the World Trade Center. We knew that whenever a pastor builds a new sanctuary, it seems that Satan sends all his efforts directly to the pastor's family and leadership in the church to bring destruction. The reason for this is that he does not want anything used to spread the gospel of Jesus Christ. That is what a new church sanctuary does! As a result of this knowledge, my family and our church family doubled down on prayer and fasting.

After the 9/11 attacks, we experienced vast cost overruns due to new building codes, fire retardants, and increases in building materials. We experienced turmoil in church families and watched as businesses failed. We faced spiritual battles on every side, or so it seemed, but we still pressed on because we knew this was not a flesh and blood battle. We fought and fought, never knowing that before the new sanctuary was completed, our greatest battle was on the horizon within our own family.

We knew our daughter was struggling. As a pastor's daughter, it had become quite easy for her to look at others and see their double standards; she was simply unable to make excuses for them. She had her own failures as she grew, but her failures were made much larger in her mind as others pointed their fingers in her direction. One day, her failures progressed past the point of failure, and she became a prodigal. As she lived her prodigal life, the Lord assured me that it was not about us, the church, the building program, our parenting, or our own spiritual lives, but her own walk with Him.

There are times when the discernment of the Holy Spirit does not share with us all that is going on in the lives of those we love because it is not about us. Sometimes, the Holy Spirit waits and allows that person we love to correct their behavior with His conviction and His help. Remember, it is not about you. It is about them and their walk.

Jordan's Story

There I was, lying on the floor of my ground loft apartment with a bottle of prescription sleeping pills and a liter of alcohol. My life was in shambles. It felt like standing up to move forward would deepen the shards of broken glass in my bare feet as I walked into self-inflicted failure. It seemed as though I had no options other than to put everyone out of their misery from the pathway of destruction I had created. Confronting the pain of trying to go back and repair all that I had broken was NOT an option. It was too hard, too painful, and required too much effort. There weren't any bridges left to burn. I had destroyed everything. There was no strength within me and nothing to pull from.

This wasn't supposed to be me. This wasn't supposed to be my life. How did I get here?

From a young age, I always felt like the Lord had marked me "for such a time as this" (see Esther 4:14). I loved being in the presence of the Lord and grew up seeing miraculous signs and wonders. Because of the environment my parents cultivated in our family home and ministry life, I was daily privy to the events people would travel far and wide to experience. My dad would often refer to me as his first associate pastor because I would visit hospitals with him, pray for people at the altar, love on newborn babies, celebrate at weddings, and comfort those during times of grief. In those early years of my parents' first ministry as lead pastors, the church had not yet grown to financially support additional staff. My dad took advantage of this and took me everywhere with him on his pastoral calls.

As I got older, my love for people and ministry deepened. I began to lead worship in my youth ministry, participate in dramatic productions at church, and go on every foreign missions trip in which I was able to participate. I loved being able to experience how Jesus transformed people's lives. When it was time for me to go to college, I decided that I wanted to go to Bible school so I could be in full-time ministry.

My first year in Bible college was fun but eye-opening. I had the opportunity to help lead worship on a travel team that ministered almost every weekend. The first-year students were not allowed to date but were encouraged to focus on their relationship with the Lord. I watched as friends of mine would sneak around and break the rules. Of course, I looked down on them with my holier-than-thou attitude and said, "A relationship born in rebellion will not last." At the end of my first year, the school was going through a very tumultuous transition of leadership. Students began to choose sides, and the entire school was divided.

On the night of graduation, a first-year couple came to the girl's dorm and said, "Hey, Jordan, watch this." They proceeded to fondle each other in front of me as if to say, "Screw you and your legalism." That summer was a much-needed break from everything that was happening.

> **Promises were left unfulfilled, and it seemed as if God had forgotten about me.**

As my sophomore year approached, the new school leadership met with me to discuss my ministry focus and leadership position. It seemed as if everything was in place for me to step into what I felt I was called to pursue. When school began a few weeks later, things had completely shifted. The very people who broke the rules and caused division were put into leadership positions above me. In my immaturity, I didn't understand and was jaded with a gaping hole of injustice for everything that had transpired. Promises were left unfulfilled, and it seemed as if God had forgotten about me. I had been faithful and honorable but then left in a cave and forgotten. I began to deal with pain and rejection like I had never experienced before. As the year progressed and transgressions were blatantly committed against me, my demeanor shifted to a nonchalant attitude. Why should I strive to live and lead in a certain way when I am being overlooked and my enemies are waiting for the day I will fail? And that's when the trap was set.

By this time, I was primed for the fury of hell with all the nonsense that was taking place in my personal, academic, and ministerial life. I ended up meeting a guy through a good friend at a young adult gathering. As a naive nineteen-year-old girl, I thought it was a great idea to date a guy ten years older who had recently been divorced and was a father to a three-year-old child. Now, I'm not saying that those individuals are unqualified, but as someone who had never experienced those things, that's not who I needed to date. Well, we were sneaking around with each other, and then my dad found out what was going on. Not only was his precious firstborn daughter dating someone he had never met, but I was also failing in my classes at school. I was kicked out of school, and my dad was the one who did it. I later found out that the school administration tried to reason with my dad for another alternative. My dad's response was, "If the standards of integrity don't apply to my family, they cannot apply to anyone."

When I was kicked out of Bible school, I moved back in with my parents. Part of the stipulations in my moving back home was that I would sever ties with my boyfriend and get a job. I always had a knack for networking, so I was able to land an amazing job at a marketing agency working with business owners. The money I was earning was that of a senior-level management position, but I was only nineteen years old. I had almost anything I wanted at my disposal, but there was a war raging inside of me between what I should do and giving up altogether. The heartache grew bigger and bigger as I used work and success to medicate the emptiness within me. Eventually, I reconnected with my boyfriend and began making future plans with him. While my parents were away on a ministry trip, I moved out of their home in a dramatic exodus to which they had no prior knowledge. That is when my prodigal life began.

Sometimes I think people can romanticize sex, drugs, and certain lifestyles when they share how Jesus delivered them. It seems like the more shock and awe they can offer, the more amazing the miracle of deliverance in their lives. For the purpose of this story, I don't even want to glorify how the enemy ruled my life or give you a step-by-step dissertation of the details of my prodigal season. I was living in sin and willfully rebelling against everything I knew to be righteous.

During my time away from home, I said and did some horrible things to my family that I wish I could take back. More importantly, I wish there was a magic pill I could give everyone to wipe THEIR memory clean! I remember one summer day (a few months before I returned home) my dad called me. As I answered the phone, I braced myself for what I perceived the phone call would entail—telling me how I had ruined something or how my actions were wreaking emotional havoc on a family member's well-being. Instead, I answered the phone to a father who had been weeping for me.

> **In one thirty-second conversation, my father had completely disarmed me with the love of his Father's heart.**

He said, "Hello, sweetheart. Please don't hang up the phone, but I just wanted to tell you that I love you and I miss you. Will you please come over to the house and just let me make you a strawberry milkshake? You can leave and go back to wherever you are, but I just want to give you a hug."

Wait a second! That wasn't fair! In one thirty-second conversation, my father had completely disarmed me with the love of his Father's heart. Up until that point, nothing could disassemble the wall I had built to protect my mind, will, and emotions. Something had changed within my father. That is when my emotional and spiritual fort's exterior began to fall. I knew my dad always loved me, but his heart was postured in vulnerable humility to see me back in his arms.

To this day, if you speak with any of my dad's closest friends who walked with him during my prodigal time, you will hear a resounding pattern of how the Lord softened his heart in different areas of his life and how it changed him for the better. I wish I could tell you that after that phone call, I dropped everything and went back home, but that is not the case. My response to Dad was nothing more than, "I can't," and I hung up the phone as fast as I could. There was so much for me to process. Not only did I feel my dad's love for me in a different way, but I felt my heavenly Father's love pursuing me in a way I had never experienced. But I still wasn't ready to surrender. I felt like I had something to prove, but I couldn't find exactly what that was.

As the months progressed, some strange events happened. I was almost killed in a car accident on the interstate, a man tried to rape me in a community pool bathroom, and I was stalked by another crazy man who found out where I was living. My relationship with my boyfriend was deteriorating, and I began to feel hopeless. All the efforts in substantiating my decisions and justification for my hurt and pain became unfounded. I had almost landed at the rock bottom. This is when the Lord began to move in my life.

I remember having to go back to my hometown for some business meetings. I stopped in a local fast-food establishment and saw one of my dad's staff members, Scott Creswell, eating lunch. Instead of writing me off and pretending I didn't exist, he gave me a hug, told me he loved me, and paid for my meal. Then, another ministry intern, Kiley Callaway, asked if he could take me out for dinner. He prefaced the invitation by saying, "This is not a date, and I don't want anything other than to see how you are doing." He met me at the restaurant with a dozen roses and sat there during the entire meal, telling me how valuable and loved I was. He encouraged the destiny of God upon my life—all while seeing me in my mess. But still, I wasn't ready to surrender.

After about two months of these wild and crazy life events, the last thing I was clinging to (my job) began to dwindle away. That is when I found myself in my loft apartment about to end it all. The day I moved out of my parents' home, I threw away EVERYTHING that reminded me of Jesus or what I was passionate about doing for His kingdom. This included journals, pictures, books, and most importantly, all my music. In my perspective, it had all been a waste because I served the Lord, and nothing had worked out for me. In my arrogance, I was determined to try to hurt God for what He had allowed to happen to me. As I lay on the floor, with my bottle of prescription sleeping pills and a liter of alcohol, I turned on some music, so I could hopefully die in comfort. During that time, music streaming was just beginning to emerge, and the radio or CD player played all your music. As I turned on the music, "Why" by Nichole Nordeman began to play. I know that moment was supernatural because I didn't have any Christian music in my apartment, yet my CD player played that song. As the song played, it felt like all the strange events that happened in the previous months had led up to this point. I physically felt the love of the Father as I heard Nichole Nordeman singing these words:

And it said, "Father, why are they screaming?
Why are the faces of some of them beaming?
Why are they casting their lots for my robe?
This crown of thorns hurts me more than it shows.
Father, please, can't you do something?
I know that You must hear my cry.

I thought I could handle a cross of this size.
Father, remind me why.
Why does everyone want me to die?
Oh, when will I understand why?"
"My precious Son, I hear them screaming.
I'm watching the face of the enemy beaming.
But soon I will clothe you in robes of my own.
Jesus, this hurts me much more than you know,
But this dark hour, I must do nothing,
Though I've heard your unbearable cry.
The power in your blood destroys all of the lies;
Soon you'll see past their unmerciful eyes.
Look, there below, see the child
Trembling by her father's side.
Now I can tell you why ...
She is why you must die."[2]

I began to weep, listening to the words of the song. Then something even more powerful happened to me. I became physically paralyzed to proceed with plans to end my life. I sat there angry that I couldn't move but then realized how much I missed Jesus.

The wall I had built to surround my emotional fortress of pain completely crumbled. The Lord reminded me of why He sacrificed Himself for me and the pain He willingly endured all for my benefit. I sat there thinking about His sacrifice and how the emotional pain of betrayal and rejection probably exceeded any physical pain He endured. And here He was, still chasing after me with all the yuck I had thrown in His face. Jesus still wanted

---

[2] Nichole Nordeman, vocalist, "Why?" released Jan 1, 2007, track #14 on *Recollection: The Best of Nichole Nordeman*, Sparrow Records.

me regardless of the horrendous choices I had made. Maybe my earthly father could extend that same grace and love. Maybe that's what he was trying to extend to me when he wanted to make me that strawberry milkshake. Maybe, just maybe. . . .

Needless to say, by the grace of God, I did not end my life that day. Over the next few days, I struggled, but the Lord continued His pursuit of me. My walls had crumbled, and I was receptive to seeing how the Lord wanted to intervene in my life.

This next stage became a pivotal point that changed the trajectory of my life. I have to say, there is something to be said for grandparents who will storm the gates of hell for their grandchildren. I have been blessed to have godly grandparents on both sides of my family. During my prodigal time, my maternal grandparents did not enable my lifestyle or the decisions I made to push people away. Instead, Papa (my maternal grandfather) would frequently call and write me letters in an effort to remind me of who I was created to be.

A few days after my attempted suicide, Papa called me. As soon as I saw that it was him calling, I answered the phone crying. As I sobbed, all I could say was, "Take me home." At that point, I didn't even know if he could understand me, but I heard him!

His response was, "I'm coming to get you."

He and my nana got in the car and drove to get me out of my mess. I remember frequently calling Papa and Nana on their way to pick me up to see how much longer they would be. It felt like I was in the fight of my life just to get home. I knew that if I could get home, I would be okay. It would be a hard recovery, but I would be safe and in the arms of my family. I asked Papa not to tell my dad that he was bringing me home. In the back of my mind, I thought that if he didn't tell my parents, they wouldn't be able to reject me.

Even through everything the Lord had brought in my life to show me otherwise, I was still struggling with rejection and unworthiness. When we arrived at my parents' house, Papa called Dad to tell him to come outside. When my parents walked around the corner of the outside sidewalk and saw me, they didn't see their screw-up daughter who tried to ruin their lives ... NO! All they saw was that their daughter had come home. I was received with the biggest embrace. In between their tears and embrace, all I could hear was both of my parents praying and thanking God that I had come home. It was a very powerful encounter!

I had missed so much in my time away from the Lord, but my heavenly Father was about to show me how restoration works in His kingdom. The week I came home just happened to be missions week at my parents' church. In my parents' ministry, this was viewed as the most important time of the year. Every financial decision, conference, or scheduled event was centered around this one week. It determined how the ministry would impact the world for Jesus for the following year. As I participated in those meetings, I became extremely conflicted. I wanted to have a part in reaching the world, but I felt so unqualified after everything I had done. During that week, I made the difficult decision to go back and finish Bible college. It was a humiliating choice because I would have to face the same people I had previously deceived.

As I went back to school, the Lord allowed me to walk through some humbling experiences that were very much needed. I saw the Lord restore the relationship with my family and build back the trust that seemed forever lost.

Selfishness, immaturity, and pride and arrogance in my life are what initiated my prodigal season. Instead of allowing the Lord to work things out of me that would destroy my life, I allowed the enemy to establish a root of bitterness in me because of hurt and pain from perceived rejection. Were things said and done to me that were wrong? Yes, but that never justified my actions. Instead, it brought more destruction in my life than it did to the people who brought the hurt and pain. Not every individual who has walked through a prodigal season has experienced it the way I did, but those events and experiences were prominent factors in mine.

Sometimes, your fight will look different than what you think.

To those who have a prodigal, my words for you are simple, but I pray they will have a profound impact on your journey to see that loved one come home. Keep fighting. You are the only one who knows them the way you do. You might be the only one fighting, and you might be the only one who hasn't given up on them, but KEEP FIGHTING. Sometimes, your fight will look different than what you think. Sometimes, the fight will be setting your face as a strong steel tower so that you will not waver, even when your prayers are misaligned with your reality.

Make the phone call. Send the text. Write the letter. Stand strong and keep your heart postured in humble vulnerability. Remember, you are the Father's heart of love.

You are the representation of the Father to your prodigal. Our intent, when trying to reach any prodigal, should be to point them to our heavenly Father and not to our own objectives. There were so many physical things the Lord did in my life that mirrored who God is as a Father. He used my dad's strawberry milkshake, Scott Creswell's kindness, and Kiley's roses to show HOW He loved me and that He wanted nothing in return but my heart. Your prodigal may be a child, a sibling, a spouse, or even a parent. Whoever they are, remember that you are God's representation of HIM in their lives.

In the body of Christ, there has been a significantly blurred line between how people become the love of Jesus to those lost in sin versus the acceptance of someone's lifestyle choices. While efforts may be with pure intent, we must adhere to the infallible Word of God for guidance in handling a prodigal. I have seen many parents enable their loved ones to stay where they are and even PUSH them deeper into their pit. This enablement is disguised as "love." Love does not equal acceptance. You cannot be fearful of risking the relationship over righteousness. This is the enemy's trickery in full play! Jesus ate meals with a prostitute, but He didn't have sex with her. We love people where they are, but we don't validate them in their mess. This enables a person to stay in bondage without experiencing true freedom.

Why am I mentioning this in my testimony of redemption? I believe the enemy wants to convolute the testimony of Jesus by distorting love as acceptance that validates people to stay in sin. He uses this compromise of our efforts by trying to be "relatable."

To those who are prodigals, you aren't so far gone that the Lord will stop trying to reach you. I pray that you have an encounter with Jesus that will change the trajectory of your life. Remember that just because you decide to come home doesn't mean the enemy of your soul will lie down and let you go without a fight. There will be times when it may seem that it's harder to stay than it would be to leave. You can do hard things because the Jesus within you REALLY is greater than he who is in the world. Certain events happened to me right after I came home that were so unbearable it made me want to drop-kick someone into infinity!

It had been about a year since I had gone to church. My first time back in church was at a mission's banquet. Following the familiar pattern of ministry servitude, I offered to help clean up after the banquet. I stepped up onto a table to take down some decorations and heard someone yelling at me, "Jordan, you need to get off that table. Your table dancing days are over!" What?!? Did someone just say that to me at a church event and in front of about a hundred other people who were helping to clean up? Later that weekend, a board member came up to me and said, "Looks like you got a second chance. Don't screw it up this time." Then a couple weeks after I got back into Bible school, a ministry student came up to share how things were better when I wasn't around, but they could learn to live with the fact that I was back. These could have been really devastating blows, but I decided not to put any weight on what these people said to me. After everything I had been through, I knew this was another ploy for me to pick up an offense and carry pain to detract from what the Lord wanted to do in my life. Satan has no new schemes other than recycling what he's already tried to accomplish. WE decide how we receive or reject things thrown in our faces. I knew what it was like to live without Jesus and never wanted to be in that place again.

My life has not been without the valleys or the mountains. I'm still walking out some different seasons and have not reached the full testimony of what Jesus has accomplished in my life. That's another story for a different time, but I now know a side of Jesus that chases me down regardless of where I am. That is not a free pass to abuse His grace but a knowing that His redemption holds me when I falter.

As I write this story, I have some joyful chaos happening all at one time. My three-year-old nephew, Jase, is running around my house asking for "Queenie" to make some popcorn, eat some marshmallows, and turn on a movie for us to watch. I am also preparing to pick up my other nephew, Shiloh, so we can grab some lunch. Scott Creswell (aka "Father Scott") just texted to check in on how life is going. When I told him he was in my story, he reminded me again of how I was in his story and how much he loves me. Mom is blowing up my phone for me to finish this so we can send it off to the publisher, and I just finished closing one of the biggest deals of my career that will fund several missions projects. This craziness may seem mundane to an outsider, but to me, it shows the restoration and redemption of Jesus at work in my life.

When you or your prodigal decide to come back home, you have a Father waiting with open arms—and maybe even a strawberry milkshake!

Parent's Prayer

Heavenly Father, it would be easy for me to blame myself for all the failures of my children. Some of it may be my fault because I am human, and I am not perfect. However, I cannot take full responsibility for their actions. Help me to remember that. Help me to help my children learn to rise from failure and walk forward into victory, and help me to do the same. Forgive me for thinking it is all about me when it is really all about You and their walk with You. In Jesus's name. Amen.

Chapter 4

Leaving Home: The Prodigal's Journey

Luke 15:11-19 and 22-32 say:
Jesus continued: "There was a man who had two sons. The younger one said to his father, 'Father, give me my share of the estate.' So he divided his property between them.

Not long after that, the younger son got together all he had, set off for a distant country and there squandered his wealth in wild living. After he had spent everything, there was a severe famine in that whole country, and he began to be in need. So he went and hired himself out to a citizen of that country, who sent him to his fields to feed pigs. He longed to fill his stomach with the pods that the pigs were eating, but no one gave him anything.

When he came to his senses, he said, "How many of my father's hired servants have food to spare, and here I am starving to death! I will set out and go back to my father and say to him: Father, I have sinned against heaven and against you. I am no longer worthy to be called your son; make me like one of your hired servants...."

But the father said to his servants, "Quick! Bring the best robe and put it on him. Put a ring on his finger and sandals on his feet. Bring the fattened calf and kill it. Let's have a feast and celebrate. For this son of mine was dead and is alive again; he was lost and is found." So they began to celebrate.

Meanwhile, the older son was in the field. When he came near the house, he heard music and dancing. So he called one of the servants and asked him what was going on. "Your brother has come," he replied, "and your father has killed the fattened calf because he has him back safe and sound."

The older brother became angry and refused to go in. So his father went out and pleaded with him. But he answered his father, "Look! All these years I've been slaving for you and never disobeyed your orders. Yet you never gave me even a young goat so I could celebrate with my friends. But when this son of yours who has squandered your property with prostitutes comes home, you kill the fattened calf for him!"

"My son," the father said, "you are always with me, and everything I have is yours. But we had to celebrate and be glad, because this brother of yours was dead and is alive again; he was lost and is found."

As parents, we are often blind-sided when we realize our child has become a prodigal. There may have been some warning signs, but the journey to becoming a prodigal is often a slow, hidden journey with many small decisions along the way that do not seem wrong at the beginning. Yet, the decisions they make are wrong, not based on the Word of God, not what they have been taught, and not what we see as good decisions. Maybe it is difficult to detect those unwise decisions simply because they haven't been caught or exposed.

A little disobedience, a little "white lie," fudging on curfew by only a few minutes, going somewhere they are not supposed to go (but who will ever know?), taking a little bit of money with the intention of paying it back but knowing the parent will never miss it, and so on. The bad decisions may never be discovered or addressed, and then the bad decisions become huge decisions that lead to destruction. The child makes excuses and then feels they deserve whatever is due to them.

Wouldn't it be nice if we could make all the decisions for our children as they grow and know that they will accept and abide by those decisions? Unfortunately, making their decisions does not foster their personal, spiritual, and emotional growth.

Parents must teach their children to make good decisions. It does not just happen. When our children were growing up, we tried to give them opportunities to make simple decisions. Do you want a cookie or a piece of candy? You cannot have both. Do you want to go to the party or stay home and go swimming with the family? As they grew, their decision-making became more important.

When Danielle was a sophomore in high school, we started a Christian high school at our church. Danielle told me she wanted to "try it out." After much discussion, I finally told her that she couldn't "try out" schools. She could "try out" Coke or Pepsi or different styles of clothing, but education was a major decision. She would need to make the decision and stick with it for the remainder of her high school years. She only had two years of high school left, and once she made this decision, it would be final. She changed schools, and it was the correct decision for her. She excelled and enjoyed her last two years.

Whenever my grandson gets into trouble, my daughter tells her toddler that he made a bad decision. She then has him tell her why the decision was a bad decision and what would have been a better choice. It is an ongoing process throughout childhood and adulthood for us to look at our own decisions and realize that there may have been a better choice for a better outcome. It is part of learning to grow up and become healthy, functioning adults. The key is learning to assess our decisions and determine if they were the correct ones or if we could have done better.

You can unknowingly help your prodigal become a prodigal.

What brings a child who has been raised in a Christian home to walk away from the tenets of faith? It may not be a conscious decision, but it is a decision. There may be various reasons, but the journey to a prodigal lifestyle always begins with hidden desires. The father of the prodigal in Scripture gave him whatever he wanted. We never see, nor is it inferred, that he lacked for anything while he was in his father's household.

The Journey of a Prodigal Always Begins With Their Hidden Desires

The younger one said to his father, "Father, give me my share of the estate." So, he divided his property between them.—Luke 15:12

Your prodigal is not going to come out and tell you what they want to do until they are pretty sure they can do exactly what they want to do. In fact, you can unknowingly help your prodigal become a prodigal. The Bible says that when this son went and asked the father for the goods that were to be given to him—his share of the inheritance—the father gladly gave it to him. The father could have had many reasons for giving his son the property. We don't know what they were. We only know that the father divided his property between the two sons. I think it is interesting that the son asked for something that didn't even belong to him, something he had never worked for and should only have been available to him after his father's death: an inheritance. Another interesting point is that the son was not entitled to anything at this time of his life. By requesting his inheritance, he was, in essence, saying that he wished his father was already dead, so he could inherit.

Maybe the prodigal had everything he desired and then more. Maybe he never had to work for anything in his father's household. We really don't know. What we do know is that because he asked for what did not belong to him, the prodigal had become covetous of what belonged to his father and his older brother. No doubt, the father had no idea of what was in his son's heart.

I can tell you as a parent, that had the father known what that son was up to, there is no way he would have ever given the son his inheritance at the time he asked for it. No godly father would have ever equipped his son to leave home, live riotously, spend everything he had, and become a pauper and a pig feeder. Jesus told us this story of a wise father, a father with great wisdom, great compassion, and great love. He had all these wonderful qualities yet didn't pick up on the hidden desires of the prodigal.

Once the prodigal had decided to leave, the father didn't try to stop him. This is a very important part of the story and an important part of the pathway of the prodigal. If they are not going to listen to what God says, they will not listen to what you say. The Holy Spirit has already been convicting them, leading them, and trying to guide them into doing the right thing. However, they are not listening. When they decide to go, it is time to let them go. Sometimes, you must release them to go their own way. By trying to make them stay, they will make your life miserable. They will make your home chaotic, and they will influence any younger children in your home. They may even turn your home into a pigpen. Once they leave, they will find that life outside of your home, outside the protection of Father God, is not what they envisioned.

All of us, as parents, want our children to do well and succeed. The Lord showed me that a parent can condemn himself for not picking up on the prodigal's hidden desire. If we are not careful, we can fall into that trap of condemnation and disallow the Holy Spirit to work in and deal with the life of the prodigal.

Once upon a time, I thought I knew all the answers about raising children; I could tell you how to do it, tell you what the Word says, and tell you if you do what the Word says, nothing will ever happen to your family. It sounded good, but throughout my time in ministry and after having children, I have learned through a series of events that God never takes away a person's moral choice. As a parent, you can try to guide moral choice, but you cannot take it away. As parents of prodigals, I want to lift that burden from your life and let you know that although your child may have deceived or fooled you, you are not alone. The father of the prodigal was also fooled, and although our sin does not fool our heavenly Father . . . He does have a prodigal world.

The Journey of a Prodigal Always Takes Him to a Foreign Country

When you have a prodigal, he or she will do things, go places, and say things they have never done before. Their actions are totally out of character with what they have ever said or done. To go to a far country means to experience things they have never experienced before. They may be adapting to a different mindset or a different culture. It doesn't always mean that they will turn their backs on what they know is right and true or that there is complete rebellion in their hearts. However, when they turn their backs on the Lord, there is another set of rules that we as parents must follow if we ever want the prodigal to come home or return to their faith.

Someone once said that sin will take you further than you meant to go, keep you longer than you meant to stay, and cost you more than you ever meant to pay. Going to a far, unknown country may seem like a fun journey at the beginning, but we never know what the end of it will be. There IS pleasure in sin for a season, but seasons come and go, and there is always death and brokenness in the winter.

If we are not careful, the enemy will manipulate us parents. In an effort to be kind and merciful, we may hinder the work of God in their lives. Sometimes, we must take a step back from our parenting and allow God to do what He needs to do in the life of our prodigal.

We came home from an event, and our daughter's car was in the driveway. That was not so unusual because she often came home from college on the weekends to do her laundry and raid the pantry. We called her name, but when she did not answer, we assumed she was napping. After all, her schedule was quite grueling. We gave her a couple of hours and heard nothing, so we decided to wake her. When we walked into her room, we found that during our time away that morning, she had moved out and taken all her personal items with her except for her car. It was in our name, and she knew we would never allow her to take it on a prodigal journey.

She was our first prodigal child, and one of the hardest things we had to do was let her go. She was an adult and had chosen to walk away from our home, from the things of God, from the call of God on her life. We did not know where she had gone or who she was with. We didn't know how she would survive, only that she was gone. We couldn't follow because we didn't know where to start. We couldn't protect her because she had chosen to come out from under our protection. We did not know how long her prodigal journey would last or how far it would take her. We only knew that we needed to stay home and anticipate her return. We had to allow her to face the consequences of her actions and the waste those actions would inevitably produce.

I mentioned in an earlier chapter that when our children were growing up, I had always prayed that if they were going to struggle with their relationship with the Lord, they would struggle while they were in our home. I knew we could offer them the covering and protection of our prayers as they struggled. This child of ours had waited until adulthood to struggle and walk away from us, her relationship with her heavenly Father, and our spiritual covering. In my prayers and petitions before God in the coming months, I began to understand that this was not about us but about her relationship with Him. God needed to prove to her that He was a God of first, second, and unlimited chances. He was her Father, and although we wanted to protect her, she needed Him on her journey into the foreign country.

The Journey Always Produces Waste

Not long after that, the younger son got together all he had, set off for a distant country, and there squandered his wealth in wild living.—Luke 15:13

If you have a prodigal, there will be waste. There will be waste of time, waste of talent, and waste of money, morals, a good name, and reputation. There will be a trash can continually collecting waste. That's what a prodigal does.

Before a baby can talk, she has her own means of communication. What does the baby do when she's hungry? She cries, often loudly. Until you put a bottle in that baby's mouth, she will continue to cry. Why? Because that's what babies do at a young age. When she produces waste, she will cry. She will continue to cry until the waste is cleaned up. When you have a prodigal in your life and your home, there may be crying, yelling, and a lot of waste.

The once-valuable time and once-adhered-to timetable will no longer be important. They don't arrive on time or don't arrive at all. Upper education and scholarships may be lost. Assignments are forgotten or ignored. Jobs may be lost. Debt may be accrued. Trust is gone. People no longer believe what he or she says they will do because they do not follow through. This may just be the beginning of the journey into waste.

> **They can make this choice if they see where they are headed and care enough to stop.**

The waste is going to be hurtful. It will be embarrassing. You will wonder what in the world they are thinking, what they are doing, and what happened to their brains. You can get the biggest dump truck in the world and try to go after them and clean up the waste they produce. You may try to make sure no one sees it. You can try to hide it and try repeatedly to help them. Unfortunately, it's not going to do any good because the prodigal is going to continue to produce waste until something happens to change the prodigal. Ultimately, that is what we want: change in the prodigal. At this point, change is still possible before the journey ensues. They can stop the journey of waste before they walk into famine and want. They can make this choice if they see where they are headed and care enough to stop.

The Journey Will Always Produce Famine and Want

After he had spent everything, there was a severe famine in that whole country, and he began to be in need. —Luke 15:14

The prodigal began to be in want because there was a severe famine in the land. He became hungry because he spent everything he had. His friends were gone. Those with whom he had partied were gone. He still had needs, but no one was there to meet them. He had turned his back on his family and walked away from how he had been raised. His lifestyle had produced waste. His journey had led him into famine and want. At any point in time, the prodigal could have repented and taken the road back home. He could have looked at how bad his life had become, and he could have changed. He didn't. He had no money, no friends, no food, no parties to attend, no place to go, and he still did not repent or seek restoration. Maybe his heart and his eyes were blinded to the reality of his life, or maybe his pride was still too great. Regardless of the reason, he remained in his sinful, rebellious state.

This is often the point where we fail in dealing with the prodigal: If you have a prodigal in your home, maybe a family member, a friend, or a distant loved one, he must experience famine and want, or there will be no restoration. When the prodigal is on his journey and producing waste, if he does not change, there will come a point in his life where famine and want will come. The restoration of your prodigal will not happen during the famine or while they are in want because, at that stage, they are not ready for what we want: restoration with God. We cannot force restoration, no matter how much we may want it. We cannot make them come to that point. It can't happen just because we want it to. Too often, we want to rush the process. Jesus tells us in this passage that there is a process that prodigals must go through. They were raised to know right, but suddenly and unexpectedly, they began going in a different direction. It is the pathway of a prodigal.

This is where tough love kicks in. Do you love your prodigal enough to watch them in their want, in their need, in their pigpen? Do you love them enough to sit back and watch them wrestle to break their cycle of rebellion and seek restoration on their own? Remember, we don't just want them at home. We want their relationship with God restored, and we cannot make that happen. The Holy Spirit draws them into His embrace, not us.

The Journey Leads to a Decision-Making Process

So he went and hired himself out to a citizen of that country who sent him to his fields to feed pigs. He longed to fill his stomach with the pods that the pigs were eating, but no one gave him anything.

When he came to his senses, he said, "How many of my father's hired men have food to spare, and here I am starving to death!"—Luke 15:15-17

We all make daily decisions. Most of the decisions we make are simple: get out of bed, eat, have our devotions, spend time with the Lord, exercise, pay bills, etc. Some of the decisions we make can be life-changing or life-altering. Going places and doing questionable things can lead us into sinfulness that will affect a large portion of our lives. When the prodigal of Luke 15 left home, he would have never imagined that he would one day feed pigs and starve to death in a faraway country.

Most of our decisions have the potential to be either good or bad. We choose. More than likely, the prodigal in Luke 15 did not throw away everything he had been taught as soon as he left home. It was a gradual descent. A bit of compromise here and there, and then one day, he was feeding pigs. This was the bottom of the barrel, so to speak, for a Jewish aristocrat. Pigs were and still are considered the most unclean of all animals. They live in dirt and mud, and they stink horribly.

When I was a girl of about ten years old, our neighbors had pigs. Occasionally, my mom or dad would send me over to their pigpen to give them some garbage, mostly food scraps. Pig slop. The pigs loved it, but I hated it! I can still remember my mother saying, "It's time to go feed the neighbor's pigs." I tried to disappear, but she inevitably found me. As soon as I got close to the pen, I could hear them squealing as if they were being injured. The closer I got, the louder and smellier it became. There was a distinct odor every time the wind blew a certain way. Garbage, pig slop, mud, and excrement all mixed together to create one big smelly mess. As soon as they saw me with the bucket in my hands, those mud-covered nasty pigs would try to climb out of the pen to get the slop I had in my bucket. I was quite afraid they would one day succeed! I held my breath and threw the slop into the trough as quickly and precisely as I could. It seemed the nastier it was, the more they liked it. Heaven forbid I accidentally let go of the bucket and throw it too! I don't know how I would have ever gotten it back because I knew I wasn't going into that pen!

As soon as I was finished slopping the hogs, I ran home, blew my nose, changed my clothes, and washed my hands and my feet, just in case anything got on me. Although I hated the smell of the pigs and their enclosure, it never dampened my love for bacon or sausage. In fact, if anything, it increased my love for both because I just imagined it came from the biggest, nastiest, meanest sow in the pen.

I cannot imagine anyone finding pig slop edible, much less desiring to eat it. That is the problem with sin and living a prodigal lifestyle. Things that were once something a prodigal would never consider doing become the norm, and he becomes blinded to the horror of it all.

A prodigal's decision-making is a three-part process.

The initial decisions are bad decisions. Feeding pigs is not a job you want to put on your resume. "I want to grow up and slop the hogs." Here is this young man who had everything going for him; he rebelled against his father and was now standing in the middle of the pigpen, possibly on a hot summer day, slopping the hogs. This is where parents and loved ones can interfere—we want to give them a handout in the pigpen before they are truly ready to face the reality of how far they have descended into sinfulness.

Bad decisions can lead a prodigal to the reality of truth. This aristocratic Jewish kid was in the middle of this pigpen, smelling and seeing the horror of the life he was now living. He was doing something that no self-respecting Jew, rich or poor, would ever be caught doing. Swine were considered unclean, something the Jewish people were not supposed to be around. And there he was, feeding them. As he stood there feeding the pigs, something began to happen in his heart. The Bible says he began to understand that none of his so-called friends or acquaintances really cared for him.

His physical hunger, something he had probably never experienced, shocked him into reality. This is where we truly make mistakes with our prodigals. We see our loved ones in the pigpen, slopping the hogs. They are hungry, and they are thirsty. It may be physical hunger, spiritual hunger, or emotional hunger. The initial parental reaction is to give them steak and mashed potatoes, to pay their bills, give them money, clothe them, and help them out. When you give a prodigal a steak and mashed potatoes while he is in the pigpen, you are prolonging his agony. I know this idea goes against every fiber of our nature as parents, but we cannot help the prodigal when he is in the pigpen. You cannot help him when the prodigal is slopping the hogs. You cannot help him when he is in the middle of degradation and sin. When you help the prodigal in the middle of his sin, and he is unwilling to come out of the sin, you are prolonging his pain as he avoids returning to God. You are only giving him temporary relief.

You must ask yourself some questions: "What is my main goal?" "Why am I doing this?" "Is it to make me feel better or give them temporary relief?" The answer is that it is temporary. The goal should be to get the prodigal back into the destiny of God for their life and get them functioning as God desires. If THAT is your main goal, then you must leave them alone. Every time you reach down into the pigpen and help, you delay the process once again. It is only when they come to the point of want and famine that God can begin to get their attention.

Allow me to give you a simple example. When our girls were young, we had a dinner rule that they could not say they didn't like something to eat if they had not tried it. We sat down to dinner one night, and Jordan refused her carrots. I told her she needed to taste them, and if she didn't like them, she didn't have to eat them. She refused. Loudly. All evening. Bedtime came around, and I sent her to bed, wrapped up her carrots, and put them in the refrigerator. The next morning, she came to the breakfast table very hungry, wanting her normal breakfast food. She was served carrots. Suddenly, due to her intense hunger, she was willing to try one bite so she could have her normal fare. Once she did so, she found that they were palatable, and she ate a large portion—because she was hungry enough.

> **What we want to do is reach down into that pigpen and pull our prodigal out.**

In one way, a prodigal is much like that. They must be hungry and in famine and want before they come to their senses. It hurts to watch those we love suffer in pain, but sometimes we have to leave them alone long enough for them to reach a point of understanding where their help comes from. God knows your prodigal much better than you do, and He knows what it will take to bring them back.

This is so hard for parents, grandparents, and loved ones. What we want to do is reach down into that pigpen and pull our prodigal out. However, leaving the pigpen must be the decision of the prodigal.

Have you ever tried to clean up a pig? What does the pig do when he is released? He runs for the closest mud pit, right? The pig loves to roll around in the mud and get dirty. The interesting thing is that the pig does not even know he is dirty or smelly because the mud pit has become normal. You can pull a pig out of a pigpen, clean it up, and put a bow tie on it. However, until that pig becomes domesticated, it will go back to the mud pit and roll around in the stinking, smelly mud. This is hard for some of us to understand: until that prodigal is ready to leave that pigpen, the mud pit, you are doing them no favors by feeding them as they sit in the pigsty.

The prodigal decided to leave the pigpen; he, on his own, recognized his hunger, famine, and want. He concluded that he needed to face the hard truth of his pitiful life. He knew his father treated his servants better than he was being treated in his own condition. If you are helping a prodigal, giving them things to help them survive, they will never face the hard truth of their life. There comes a time when we all must draw the proverbial line in the sand. We must all exercise tough love. If we don't, they will never experience the hunger, famine, and want that will make them see the condition of their reality.

The prodigal decided to go home because he was confronted with the truth of his humble circumstances. Some of us have tried every way possible to get our prodigal to come home. You cannot buy your prodigal home and you cannot coach your prodigal home. You cannot convince or contrive to get your prodigal to come home. The only way you can get your prodigal home is to pray them home.

That is the only way we survived: prayer. Lots and lots of prayer. Days, nights. Intercession. Lying on the floor, crying out to God, faces planted on the altar, but still moving forward in the work God had for us to do in His kingdom.

There was one day when I needed to head toward Atlanta to purchase some things for an upcoming event at the church. As I drove through the town, I prayed. I cried out to God for my prodigal and for Him to keep a hedge of protection around her. To not allow her to go into eternity without Him. As I beat the steering wheel with my fist, I told God, "I will obey you. I will do what your Word says. I will obey you." Suddenly in the quiet corners of my car, a booming voice resounded, "Yes, I know you will obey me, but when will you learn to trust me?" I knew that in all my will to obey what the Word of God told me to do, I had failed to trust that He knew what was best for my child, that He knew how to reach her and bring her back. I had to learn to trust His heart. I found that trust is not a passive but an active exercise of will. It is often something that I must cling to when circumstances convince me that obedience is the proper escape route.

Learning to trust that God will fulfill His promises is one of the hardest things to learn. This is a personal parental journey.

Parent's Prayer

Heavenly Father, I am trying, really trying to not just obey Your Word but to learn to truly trust You during this time. I know You love my child far more than I ever could. I know You see where she is and what she is doing. Although I have compassion for what she is experiencing, You have much more for her. She is wasting her gifts and learning things I never wanted her to know. She is making decisions that could affect the rest of her life. As difficult as this is for me to pray, above all else, please save her soul. Yes, I want her life to be saved, but I want her soul washed clean before she goes into eternity. In Jesus's name. Amen.

Chapter 5

The Journey Home

Your prodigal may reach the bottom. There may be a toll they have to pay. There may be pain. Your child WILL be different. The prodigal may be angry that their lifestyle didn't bring the rewards they expected. There may be personal disappointment and regret. There may be physical issues to face. There may be diseases, addictions, or consequences of an immoral lifestyle. There may be a spouse, an ex-spouse, a child, a prison sentence in the past, probation, unsavory friendships, or any number of things you never expected your child would bring. When your prodigal returns, one thing that should be present is repentance. A whole journey of repentance.

We must allow the Holy Spirit to work in the heart of the prodigal and not interfere. They must decide to leave the pigpen and start the journey of repentance. We cannot stand outside the pigpen, beckon them to come out, come home, and have a bite of good food to eat. They must be willing to repent, leave sin behind, and start over.

> *The pigpen didn't get up and leave the prodigal son. The prodigal son got up and left the pigpen. Sin will not leave you. You must get up and leave the sin.* —Dr. Tim Todd

The prodigal son knew he was lost, far away from home, and out of fellowship with his father. He even knew the way back home but had to choose it, much as the wayward soul must choose to return to fellowship with his heavenly Father. However, calling a prodigal home too soon will doom them to repeat their actions. It must be their own choice. If you keep running to grab your prodigal out of their place of sin, their pigpen, that is what you will spend the rest of your life doing. You will continue bailing them out time after time after time. There should come a time in your life when you must say you have had enough and finally trust God with your prodigal. You may not understand what is going on, but you will simply need to walk according to the Word of God and do what it tells you to do. Trusting God to lead your prodigal back home is not just an act of faith but an act of your will.

The reality of all of this is that YOU cannot change anything. Satan wants you to think that if you spend enough money and enough time on your prodigal, it will change the way things are going. He will use this to bring more frustration and pain into your home and spiritual life, and your prodigal's rebellion will consume you so greatly that you will be unable to function in other areas of your life. If Satan can do this, he not only wins the life and eternity of the prodigal, but he also destroys what God wants to do in your life.

Recently, I was talking with a young lady who grew up in our church. As we spoke about her family and how her parents were doing, I also asked about each of her siblings. Her brother was one of my favorites. There was something so very special about him, but he strayed as a young teen. I remember many times when he was arrested, came to church drunk or high, dropped out of college, and couldn't seem to keep a job. His sister told me that her parents spent all their time and a massive amount of money bailing him out of one scrape after another. Now, he is almost forty years old, has no regular job, and is only equipped to buy and sell what he finds at junk sales. He is still dependent on his parents to support him. I have wondered how much longer his parents will continue to pull him out of his pigpen and when he will truly tire of the life he is living. When will repentance prevail in his life?

Regret is defined as a missed opportunity or feeling sad or disappointed over something, but repentance takes it a step further. True repentance involves action. It is not passive. One can feel regret without ever repenting, but one can never truly repent without feeling regret. The prodigal in Luke was first regretful but chose to take action by moving forward into repentance.

> **One can feel regret without ever repenting, but one can never truly repent without feeling regret.**

Second Corinthians 7:10 tells us that godly sorrow will lead to repentance, but worldly sorrow will lead to death (author paraphrase). How many times have we heard stories of those who have made grave mistakes in their lives and lived to regret those mistakes? They begin to think they must live with their mistakes and the consequences of the mistakes, so they give up and become hopeless. Satan does not care if we are sorrowful for our mistakes and our sins. He does not care if we carry the weight of our guilt. In fact, he likes it because it is an added grief that keeps us from God. He can then use that sorrow to heap condemnation into our lives. That is worldly sorrow. The difference between condemnation and conviction is somewhat simple. The worldly sorrow and condemnation that come from Satan tell us that we are wretched, wicked, unworthy, and there is no hope for us. Satan offers us no way out of our pain. Instead, he will badger us with that pain for the remainder of our lives if we allow it.

Conviction is totally different. While we ARE wretched, wicked, and unworthy, there is hope for us. There is a way out of our pain, and it is through repentance and a relationship with Jesus Christ. That is conviction. It offers us a way out. Condemnation does not.

If we allow the Holy Spirit to work in the life of our prodigal, He will produce godly sorrow for their actions and their prodigal lifestyle. If we do not allow the Holy Spirit to work but try to rush the process, in our desire to "help," we will produce worldly sorrow. Worldly sorrow is only temporary and does not truly touch the soul. Only godly sorrow will produce sorrow and conviction that leads to repentance and change that will last.

When the prodigal was feeding the pigs, he suddenly realized that his father's servants were better off than he was. Let's backtrack a little bit. First, the prodigal journeyed to a far country.

Traveling to a far country was not a short journey in that day. The journey could take weeks, months, maybe even years. During his travels, he was spending money and living riotously. He stayed on his journey long enough to become a citizen of that country after he had spent everything he had. Maybe this was the same as becoming an indentured servant or a slave—again, not a quick process. After all this time, while feeding the pigs, the prodigal realized that he was broke, hungry, dirty, and with ceremonially unclean animals. If he had spent much time in the dregs of the filth of swine, he could have had diseases that these animals carried. It could have taken years for him to "come to himself." After he had this realization, the prodigal had to journey back home from the far country where he was living. We don't know how he got back home, only that he started the journey with repentance in his heart.

Recall Luke 15:18-19: "I will set out and go back to my father and say to him: Father, I have sinned against heaven and against you. I am no longer worthy to be called your son. Make me like one of your hired servants."

He started the journey the same way he left the pigpen: broke, hungry, dirty, and repentant. If he had no one to feed him while in the pigpen, he probably had no one to help him on his journey. We don't know if he had an extra set of clean clothes, if he had shoes on his feet, or if he even walked the journey with a clean body. Did he have food for the journey? Money? A bed or blanket for sleeping at night? Something to start a fire to keep warm? A flask for water? We only know he decided to set out for home with repentance in his heart. During the journey, he had time to think of his mistakes and all that he had wasted. He had many days to reflect. I am sure he had many regrets to ponder on. He had time to wonder about the reception he would receive when he arrived at his father's home and whether his father would even still be alive. If his father was not alive, how would his brother receive him? The questions could have been many during his journey home. Still, he journeyed, knowing he needed to repent. Restoration was questionable.

What about the mental, emotional, and spiritual battles he faced during his journey? Remember, Satan did not want to lose this prodigal. He never wants to lose a soul. We don't know what happened on the journey home. We can only speculate. The enemy may have told the prodigal many times that he would not be received well. Satan could have whispered into the heart of the prodigal that his family would tell him to leave and never return. He had shamed his father and his family, and he would not be welcomed. In his mind's eye, the prodigal may have, for the first time, remembered the pain in his father's face when he left with his inheritance. He may have also thought of his brother's anger toward him. Satan would have continuously bombarded his spirit with all the reasons not to return home. The prodigal had lost everything and had nothing *left* to lose, so he continued the journey toward home, all the while weighed down with the knowledge of his grave sin but with a heart of complete repentance.

The prodigal knew that he needed to repent if he were to continue in life. He knew he must make things right with those he had wronged, and he needed to confess his wrongs to them. Restoration is missing in our modern idea of repentance. We seem to think that all we need to do is confess our wrongs to God and move on. We forget that when we have wronged someone, we should try to correct the wrong we have done to them. Grace and mercy are wonderful things that God has given us, but we should never mistake the grace and mercy of God as a lack of responsibility for our lives. Not accepting responsibility for our actions breeds arrogance.

I was a little girl, about seven years old, when I went to a store that was owned by a family member and stole a Barbie dress that was not in the package. I don't know how much it would have cost or where it belonged, but in my mind, since it wasn't packaged, it was okay. But it wasn't. I took it home, but every time I tried to put that dress on Midge (Barbie's friend), I couldn't do it. I knew it wasn't mine. I had stolen it. I don't remember what the dress looked like or what I did with it, only that it gave me no pleasure once I had it. As Shakespeare said in *The Merchant of Venice*, I found "all that glitters is not gold."[3]

When I became an adult and realized that God had called me into ministry, the Lord reminded me of that stupid Barbie dress I had stolen and that I needed to make it right. And not just once! He reminded me again and again. I would wake up at night thinking about my wrong, my sin. I tried to make excuses: it was only worth about a dollar. What's the big deal? It probably would have been thrown away anyway. It was dirty and shopworn but it wasn't my decision to make. No one else knew about it. I even tried to tell myself it didn't really happen. I didn't take it. I dreamed it. I imagined it, but in my heart of hearts, I knew I did it. So, I wrote a letter to my family member, confessing my wrong and sinfulness, including the money for the item I had stolen. My

---
3 William Shakespeare, *The Merchant of Venice*, 2.7.

conscience was clear. I knew I had done the right thing. I had made restitution. It was finally over, and I could sleep again. It wasn't that big of a deal in the big scheme of things as far as value goes, but it was a matter of character. My character. If I wanted God to use me, I needed to learn to be faithful in the little things.

We all need to make things right between us and our brothers and sisters in Christ. In fact, we need to make things right between us and others whether they are other believers or not. It is probably more important to repent of our wrongs to those who are not believers:

Therefore, if you are offering your gift at the altar and there remember that your brother has something against you, leave your gift there in front of the altar. First go and be reconciled to them; then come and offer your gift.—Matthew 5:23-24

When my father was a young man, he came to know Christ. He didn't talk a lot about the extent of his sinfulness, only that he was not a stellar man before he came to know Christ. One story he did share was the time he stole money that did not belong to him when he was a service station attendant. After he was paid for pumping gas into cars, he put the money into his pocket instead of the cash register. After he left his job for the day and found the money in his pocket, he did not return it. He kept it, which means he stole the money from his employer. (Employee theft was a real thing even in the 1950s!) This happened more than once.

After Daddy came to know Christ, he confessed his sin to his former employer. He and his employer agreed on how much he needed to pay back, and Daddy began to make restitution. By this time, Daddy was married and had a child on the way. It took quite a while to pay the money back, as he did not have the extra money to do so, but he felt it was the right thing to do. It WAS the responsible and godly action to take. Not only did my father make things right with God, but he also made things right with his former employer. How much better off would all of us be if we made restitution for the wrongs we have committed against others, either with or without intention? We still have grace and mercy even without restitution, but restitution is evidence of our conversion and a statement of willingness to walk away from our sinfulness and go in a different direction from our former selves.

> **What is the harm in repenting, not just to God, but to those we have wronged?**

How many times have people come to know Christ and never attempted to make restitution for the wrongs they have committed against others? What message does this send to those who don't know Christ? Yes, there is grace for us, but why are we so afraid or unwilling to admit that we may have been wrong in the ways we have dealt with people? Are we perfect people? What is the harm in repenting, not just to God, but to those we have wronged?

Many years ago, a lady was at the altars of our church weeping over her sinful lifestyle and the pain she had caused for so many. She had been "the other woman" on more than one occasion.

As one of our altar workers prayed with her and counseled her through her heartache, assuring her of God's forgiveness of her sin, "the other woman" lifted her head, and the altar worker immediately recognized who she was—the woman who had destroyed the home of her parents. Our altar worker had just told her that God could forgive anything! As they faced one another, "the other woman" rose from her knees, sure she would be outed as an adulterous woman. Our altar worker had to make a quick decision to accept the woman's plea for forgiveness or continue to hold this woman responsible for the destruction of her childhood home. She chose to forgive. As they embraced one another, healing flowed, and the burden of sin and restoration was almost visible before they rose from the altar of repentance.

As someone once said, "We forgive, not because someone deserves it, but because we deserve peace." Whether you are a prodigal or a person holding unforgiveness, you need to learn to offer forgiveness, receive forgiveness, and seek restoration. Sometimes, restoration is impossible, but if there is an opportunity, we should take it.

When the prodigal determined to return home, he recognized that if his father was going to give him mercy, he needed to correct the wrongs he had committed. As he journeyed, he did not know if his efforts would be received or if they would be rejected. He only knew he needed to try.

His journey to repentance consisted of four things:

1) The prodigal made a confession of sin against God and his parents. He knew he had done wrong. He had gravely wounded his family. He recognized his sin and his arrogance and knew he needed to go home in humility. Remember,

he had started the journey home knowing he had done wrong. He probably had days, weeks, maybe even months for those wrongs to ruminate in his spirit. By asking for his inheritance early, he had essentially said his father was as good as dead to him. He didn't know if he would have the opportunity to confess his wrong to his father, but he knew he wanted to do so. He didn't know how he would be received, but he knew he had to make an effort.

2) The prodigal confessed his unworthiness. He no longer had the idea that he was worthy of any special consideration or merit. He knew he was not deserving of any honor. He just wanted to come home. He desired restoration with his family but did not know if it would happen. However, what he DID know was that he was unworthy of consideration.

3) The prodigal requested to be a hired servant. This was a very important part of his repentance. He did not want to be a slave, but he wanted to work for a living. During that time, a slave had no privileges or rights but was often treated as one of the family. By asking to be a hired servant, the prodigal was saying that he knew he did not deserve to be a part of the family, that he would have no job security, and could be released from it at any time. However, he was willing to earn his way if he was welcomed. He did not want any more handouts because of his position. His lifestyle had taken away his pride and the feeling that he was important. He no longer felt superior to others, and he had resigned himself to the fact that he was no longer a part of the family. He was destined to live a life alone. Because he was willing to come home and work for a living demonstrated that he

had a change of heart and a change of attitude. This was not just a behavioral change resulting from a decision and an action. This change was a result of the Spirit of God working in his heart.

4) The prodigal made the first move to come home. The father probably had the means and the ability to send servants to retrieve his son. He could have sent them to search for him and beg him to come home. He could have sent money and clothing for the journey. The father could have even gone to search for him and physically bring him home. However, he didn't. The father did not go and bring him home. The father did not chase him down or search for him. There is no evidence that the father did anything other than wait for the prodigal son to come to his senses and return home on his own.

> **Letting a prodigal leave is one of the most difficult things a parent can do. Praying and waiting for them to return is the second most difficult thing a parent can do.**

The father was not standing at the pigpen beckoning his son to come out. As parents, grandparents, and loved ones of the prodigal, this is probably the toughest emotional place to be, especially if you know in which pigpen your prodigal may be living. This is when your heart dies a thousand deaths, and you want to fix things, repair them, make them better. This is also when Satan will begin to manipulate your emotions. People will tell you where they saw your prodigal, what they were doing, how hard a time they are having, and may even suggest ways you can help them come home. You may become weary in the waiting.

This is exactly what Satan wants. He wants us to step in and interfere in what God wants to do in the lives of our prodigal. The spiritual power that Satan has over them must be broken by the Holy Spirit, not by us, and if we interfere, we just delay the process. We rarely understand that God is going to do much more in their lives and has something much better for them than we ever considered. God always has a better plan for our prodigal than we could imagine. Their decision to leave the pigpen must be the decision of the prodigal, not ours. They must become tired of their lifestyle, tired of their filth, tired of their want, their need, and their loneliness. They must be at the point where they are ready for repentance and restoration more than anything else in their lives. They should be at a place where they are willing to do anything to step into a right relationship with their heavenly Father.

Letting a prodigal leave is one of the most difficult things a parent can do. Praying and waiting for them to return is the second most difficult thing a parent can do. It is in the praying and in the waiting that the heavenly Father proves that He knows what He is doing and that He loves the prodigal much more than the parent ever could.

My father was from a family of six boys and one girl who lived to adulthood. The two oldest boys were drafted into military service to serve in World War II. During that time, communication was difficult and sporadic. Of course, there were no cell phones or computers, and I doubt there was a telephone in their home. No family wanted to receive a telegram or a visit from the military. If there was a visit from the military or a telegram that came to the home, it was always bad news. Two of my father's older brothers, J. W. and Fred, miraculously survived the war, both serving on the same ship and neither receiving any injuries. Once the news filtered over the radio airwaves that the war was over, the family knew Daddy's brothers were eventually coming home.

Daddy told us how his mother would stand at the door waiting for any sign of their arrival. No one knew when they would arrive, only that they were coming. Every day, for days, then weeks, my grandmother would walk to the doorway multiple times, look down the dusty country road, and stand for a few moments, watching, sighing, anticipating. All the children who were old enough were instructed to keep an eye out and let her know if they saw anyone coming. One day Papa and some of the children were working in the fields when they heard my grandmother shouting. They all ran toward the house to see her running down the road as fast as she could, waving a dishtowel over her head, shouting, "They're home, they're home! Here they come!" No one had to question what she meant as they looked and saw their brothers running toward their mom and dad for a joyous reunion.

Papa dropped his lumber-cutting equipment in the fields and ran. Granny left the food on the old wood stove, not caring if something burned as she ran toward her boys. Both were only interested in putting their arms around their sons who had been gone—their lives in danger—not knowing if they would ever see them again. There were many hugs and tears that day, and conversations continued well into the night as they all relayed the latest news of the end of the war and the local community. No one cared if there was travel dust on the boys when they arrived or if they smelled of body odor. No one questioned if they were hungry or wanted to have dinner together that evening. It was enough to know that, once again, the family was together, all were healthy, and they were able to look into each other's faces and share their love and concern for each other. They could hear their voices, touch their hands, and know that, for the moment, all was well.

I can imagine a similar reunion between the prodigal and his father. How many mornings had the father of the prodigal stepped outside his home and looked in the direction his prodigal son had journeyed the day he left those many years ago and wondered if this would be the day he returned? How many times had he come home in the evenings and looked into the distance, thinking the lone figure walking down the road might be his son? How many times had he prayed and fasted, believing God that the prayers he prayed would one day be answered and that he would see the answers to those prayers fulfilled? Would he return as the wealthy man he had been when he left with family and possessions? The father did not know how the prodigal would return, but he did know that he had to trust that God would bring him home and that prayers would be answered.

Just as the prodigal's father did not chase after his son or go looking for him, Jesus does not come to us crawling, begging, or crying for us to come back to Him; however, He is there to reach his arms around us, pick us up, lift us up, and love us when we come to Him.

Parent's Prayer

Heavenly Father, how long must I wait? How much longer will my child be away? Are You convicting them of their sin? Please help me not interfere in Your process. Please bring my prodigal to a place where he comes to himself and recognizes the pigpen where he is now living. Make him thoroughly sick of his lifestyle and his sinfulness. Bring conviction to his soul and help him to see the need for repentance. In this process, give me the stamina to see it through to the end so I can again reach my arms around my prodigal who has returned. In Jesus's name. Amen.

Chapter 6

The Return

Let's open this chapter with Luke 15:20-24:
So he got up and went to his father.
But while he was still a long way off, his father saw him and was filled with compassion for him; he ran to his son, threw his arms around him and kissed him.

The son said to him, "Father, I have sinned against heaven and against you. I am no longer worthy to be called your son."

But the father said to his servants, "Quick! Bring the best robe and put it on him. Put a ring on his finger and sandals on his feet. Bring the fattened calf and kill it. Let's have a feast and celebrate. For this son of mine was dead and is alive again; he was lost and is found." So they began to celebrate.

Have you ever been on a long journey and returned home, ready to be embraced, only to find that the one you longed to embrace does not want to embrace you? Many years ago, I traveled to

Haiti with a group of ladies for a mission trip to local villages and orphanages. Although we stayed on a compound, our water supply and electricity were limited to a few hours per day. On the last day of our stay, we all wanted to be clean and neat for our journey home. We showered and brushed our teeth; I put my hair in a baseball cap, and we headed to the airport. By the time we arrived at the airport, we were all once again sweaty and smelly, but we didn't care. We were headed home, ready to be with family, in our own country, eating our own foods, drinking our own water, and showering in our own clean bathrooms without the tarantulas and smell of acrid smoke from the landfill. (That's what we hope it was. . . .) We boarded the airplane, arrived in Atlanta, disembarked, went through customs, and were greeted by our lonely families.

I watched husbands greet their wives, and I saw the consternation on their faces as they caught a whiff of the Haitian aura surrounding us all. I suddenly realized that even with our bathing and primping, we still did not smell very good at all!

My husband pushed his way forward, and as he approached, I warned him, "I stink."

"Yes, you do, but I don't care!" He wrapped his arms around me, somewhat oblivious of the odor, only glad to have me home, safe and sound.

I wonder if the prodigal's father felt the same.

I was not a prodigal, but I knew I was missed while I was gone because of the greeting I received as I returned home: an embrace, a kiss, and a look of love in the eyes of my husband. How much more the father of the prodigal must have longed to embrace his son, regardless of the odor his son brought with him? The stench may have been overpowering but that was only the beginning. He brought home an odor of the journey, the pigsty where he had been, but he probably also brought home memories, habits, ideas, characteristics, and thought patterns he had acquired along the way. The prodigal was not the same person he was when he left. Yes, he was still the son, but he had changed. There was an odor of what he had experienced while he was gone and he needed a cleansing, not only of his heart but also his life. The cleansing had started on his journey home, but the work had likely just begun. There was still work to be done in his life—and in our lives, too.

I still do not understand how the father knew it was his son coming up the road. It is obvious to me that the father was watching and waiting for the son, but how did he know it was him? Did the father recognize his walk? Had he not physically changed at all since he had been gone, or was the father's heart so in tune with the heavenly Father that he knew it was him before the son was on his way? Maybe someone had run ahead to tell him that his son was coming down the road and to be prepared. Maybe there was such a drastic change in his physical appearance that someone had to prepare the father in advance of his arrival. In my mind's eye, I can see a broken down, emaciated, barefoot, ragged, dirty man stumbling down the road. Maybe he was so very filthy that flies were buzzing around him. But somehow, the father knew it was him, and his heart was moved with compassion.

You see, when the father saw him far off, he started running. He probably began yelling, "My son, my son, my son!" Every day the father had been standing in faith, waiting and believing that his prodigal was coming home, and when the prodigal was a long way off, the father saw him. Just by looking at his son, the father knew things had not gone the way his son had expected.

Maybe there was something distinctive in his walk as he returned. Maybe there was a dejected set of his shoulders. Maybe his head was bowed low, and he couldn't meet the eyes of his father. Remember, when he left, there was pride and arrogance. He may have strutted out the door, indicating he felt he was smarter than his father. He knew better than everyone in the family. His father was not relevant any longer. He was going to do his own thing, make his own way in the world, and show them what he was made of. However, when the prodigal returned home, the humility of God was in him. He was walking a little bit different. His chest wasn't stuck out quite as much. He was reliant and dependent on what could happen in his future. Every step he took on the road home was a step of faith, and the humility of God was being birthed in his life. Every step that he took was a step away from his sinful lifestyle. He decided to turn his back on the past. It was only after he decided to end that part of his life and walk away from it that his father was able to embrace him. Parents are often too willing to embrace their prodigals and the sinful lives they lead, not knowing that doing so invites the sin back into their homes before repentance and before God has finished His cleansing work.

The prodigal had gone to a foreign country far away. He had to walk back to the place where he would find his restoration. Every time the prodigal took a step, it was a step toward building faith in his heart. He was hoping beyond hope that there could still be restoration. Every step of the way home, he was probably practicing his speech to his father—asking for forgiveness, showing his remorse, and expressing his willingness to be a servant.

Still, in all his son's filth, disappointment, sorrow, and the changes that sin had wrought in his life, the father ran to his son, threw his arms around him, and kissed him. He made it easy for his son to repent. The father fell on his neck and kissed him. This was an act of total and complete forgiveness. The kiss said that his father held no bitterness, that the past was in the past. He didn't tell his son to go first and get cleaned up and he would then greet him properly. He forgave and accepted him back immediately, offering him love and restoration in one act: a kiss.

> **The father didn't ask anything of his son. He embraced and kissed him.**

This is part of the character of God and was an immediate offer of forgiveness, acceptance, love, and restoration. The father did not know everything that had happened to his son. We don't know whether the father asked what happened, if there was any inheritance left, or if he was sorry for all he had done. The father didn't take the time to ask if he was bringing home diseases, a bad reputation, or if law enforcement was after him. He didn't ask if he had kept the laws of God while he was gone. In fact, the father didn't ask anything of his son. He embraced and kissed him.

The father was given the privilege of showing his son who God the Father truly is. There are very few times in life that we have an opportunity to be Jesus to someone. When your prodigal comes home, you get to be a stand-in for the arms of Jesus Christ. It is your physical arms that your prodigal will feel and your forgiveness that they will first experience. Your arms need to wrap around the prodigal and your lips need to kiss that cheek. Your embrace should hold them as they weep in sorrow for their shame. They know they have caused hurt, and they are now hurting. It is in the embrace that restoration begins.

The father knew that something bad had happened and his son was willing to work his way through the restoration. The prodigal had been on a long journey and knew there was a process that he needed to walk through. He knew he was not worthy to be a son and he only wanted to receive forgiveness. He requested to become a hired servant. The father, unwilling to place his lost son in the position of a servant, elevated him back into sonship.

Once the father had embraced and kissed his son, it was evident to those around him that there was forgiveness for the things the prodigal had done. His forgiveness became more deeply evident when he commanded the servants to get a ring and robe for his son and kill the fattened calf. By asking for a robe, the father was covering his son's sin, his nakedness, and his humility. Remember, the prodigal had been living in abject poverty, and his clothing was probably shredded—not exactly the pinnacle of modesty. Everyone in the community probably already knew that the prodigal had shamed his father, but the father was not going to expose his nakedness or filth and further the son's shame. He was covering for him! By covering him modestly and giving him a ring for his finger, he gave him his total forgiveness and elevated him as a son, not a slave or a servant. It was a gesture of acceptance back into the family. He was the only one in the family who could truly offer him his place back. His mother, if she were alive, had no authority to do it. His brother, as later indicated in Scripture, was too resentful to do it. There was no other servant, no slave, no other person in the household who could bring him back into fellowship. Thus, it was up to the father to bring him back into the family, and it was his father's joy to do so.

There are some characteristics we need to know about the father of the prodigal. Although his son had essentially turned his back on the entire family and acted in arrogance and entitlement when he left, the father never gave up believing that he would one day return. He must have been diligent to intercede for his son; the evidence is found in his waiting and watching for his son's return. He had faith that if he did what he was supposed to do, his son would one day find his way back home. He had confidence in the process of standing in faith, and because he believed, it gave him courage to do exactly what God had told him to do. Every day that we do what we are supposed to do in dealing with our prodigals is a day closer to their return. There may be times that we want to do things to help our prodigal. We may want to reach out because it will help relieve our own pain and suffering, but that is not God's plan. As parents, we cannot resolve the situation and must allow the Holy Spirit to work in their lives.

Some of the greatest things that God has accomplished in my life have been through heartache and pain. It didn't feel like it at the time, but when I came through my pain as a person of faith and integrity, I knew I could stand in the midst of the storm. God used the pain to reveal Himself to me. There was intimacy with God that began to develop in my time of pain. I became sensitive to the voice of God; I began to be more compassionate and merciful. I began to see things through the eyes of my heavenly Father as never before.

That is what happened to the prodigal's father: as he stood in faith and compassion began to develop in his heart, he made it easy for the prodigal to repent when he ran to him and embraced him in forgiveness. The kiss for his son told him that he held no bitterness for all the son had done. We don't know how long they may have stood there weeping in each other's arms. We only know that healing began in their relationship as they stood together.

In the mind of the father, it was as if the son had never left.

When the father called for his servants to give his son the robe, he demonstrated that he could not only forgive but forget what the son had done. The robe was a celebration of the prodigal's return to the position of son. The robe also symbolized the restoration of his covenant with his father. In the mind of the father, it was as if the son had never left.

The father demonstrated that he had the power to restore his son as he called for a ring and shoes. The ring was a symbol of the power and authority of the family name. The shoes distinguished him from a slave. The father gave power and status back to his son.

The father also demonstrated that he had the heart to celebrate when he called for the fattened calf to be killed and for a feast to commence. He didn't just rejoice privately; he called for others to rejoice with him.

Faith will always make sacrifices, always celebrate repentance, and always celebrate life and restoration. It does not withhold love or forgiveness to make a person pay for the pain they may have caused. There is no record that the father ever did more than rejoice over the return of his son, like Luke 15:7 says, "I tell you that in the same way there will be more rejoicing in heaven over one sinner who repents than over ninety-nine righteous persons who do not need to repent."

We don't know what kinds of conversations happened after the prodigal came home. One of the things we can be sure of is that if we allow our prodigal to come home after God has brought humility into his life, the chances are that the prodigal will never return to the pigpen. He will never go back into the lifestyle of the prodigal. He will remember the pain, the degradation, and the heartache, and he will never want to revisit it. He may not want to talk about his experiences. He may never want you, as his parent, to know all that he suffered. That is his choice. You must be okay with that. In fact, it is probably better that you never know the extent of sin, suffering, and even sorrow that your prodigal experienced while living a life away from God. It is their story, not yours. Your restoration of sonship is not based on what you know. It is based on being the hands of Jesus extended toward your prodigal and offering forgiveness.

Be encouraged! One day your prodigal is going to come home. Whether your prodigal has left your physical home, left their walk with the Lord, or both, one day, they will return.

Hebrews 7:25 says, "Therefore he is able to save completely, those who come to God through him, because he always lives to intercede for them." Psalm 37:25 says, "I was young and now I am old, yet I have never seen the righteous forsaken or their children begging bread."

You need to be ready. Keep the fattened calf ready to celebrate. You may have already given up on what God has for your life and for theirs. You may have forgotten the promises that God made to you about your child. Reclaim those promises. Reclaim the dream you had for your child. One day you are going to celebrate the goodness of God as your prodigal comes home, and there will be a celebration day. Your biggest battle may be those who discourage you from believing in His promises and want you to give up on the upcoming celebration. They may think your faith looks foolish. They may be good people, loving people, kind people, or even godly people, but they will never understand what God has spoken to your heart. You must believe and stand for the promises. If you stand long enough in faith, which is the substance of things not seen, the evidence of His promises will one day spring forth. The fulfillment is coming. Refuse to give up. Remember what the Holy Spirit spoke to your heart. As long as you don't let go of the dream, it will not die. Sometimes, you may be the only one that keeps the dream alive. As long as you keep the dream alive, keep praying, and stand in faith, you'll watch the dream and promises of God live. Get ready to celebrate!

Parent's Prayer

Heavenly Father, I am waiting, watching, waiting again, standing in faith, and believing that my prodigal is going to return. I won't give up. I will keep the dream that You have given me alive in my heart, and I will trust Your promises. I will be ready to forgive, accept, love, and restore my prodigal when he returns because I know it is going to happen. I am learning to trust You in the process and will be ready to celebrate when it does. In Jesus's name. Amen.

Chapter 7

Forgiveness and Restoration

God's love for us is not based on our faithfulness. Let's return to our prodigal son.

Meanwhile, the older son was in the field. When he came near the house, he heard music and dancing. So he called one of the servants and asked him what was going on. "Your brother has come," he replied, "and your father has killed the fattened calf because he has him back safe and sound."

The older brother became angry and refused to go in. So, his father went out and pleaded with him. But he answered his father, "Look! All these years I've been slaving for you and never disobeyed your orders. Yet you never gave me even a young goat so I could celebrate with my friends. But when this son of yours who has squandered your property with prostitutes comes home, you kill the fattened calf for him!"

> *"My son," the father said, "you are always with me, and everything I have is yours. But we had to celebrate and be glad, because this brother of yours was dead and is alive again; he was lost and is found."* —Luke 15:25-32

The end. But it really isn't. That is all we are told of this story. It ends on a good note with the idea of joy and celebration, at least on the father's part. But what happened after the end of this parable? Is the celebration truly the end or is there more? Of course, the father is ecstatic that his prodigal is finally home, but the older brother is not so happy. He had no mercy. The focus of this story is usually on the horror of what the prodigal did and the faithfulness and reactions of the father when the prodigal finally returned. Very often, when we talk or read about the prodigal son and his father, we neglect to talk about the prodigal's brother.

It is obvious from the brother's reaction that he was not happy about his brother's return. He may have assumed that life would pick up where it had left off, and things would return to the way it had been before his brother left. He may have remembered the conflict, the pain, the heartache, the struggle, and the betrayal of his parent. He probably watched it for years, never knowing how to alleviate the heartache and knowing that *he* was not enough to alleviate the heartache of his father. Regardless of the reasons, which we do not know, he was judgmental when the prodigal returned. Obviously, he had never forgiven his brother for the wrong or the sin he had committed against his father and against his family. Maybe his father could forgive, but he could not. He was willing to hold his brother's past against him for as long as he deemed necessary. In his eyes, his brother's sin was unforgivable.

After reading the scripture outlining the brother's reaction, think about this: The brother came in from the fields and saw a party happening in his father's home. No one bothered to send word to him that his brother had come home. Why? Did they anticipate his reaction, or was he too far away for the servants to notify him? How would you feel if you came home to a party that you were not invited to attend? How long had the party been going on? Had it just started, or was it well underway? Was the food still plentiful, or was it all gone? Was there any food left for him? Remember: he had just come in from the fields. He was probably tired, dirty, and ready to rest after a long day's work. Instead of finding respite, he found a party. He refused to participate, refused to share in his father's joy, refused to celebrate, and acted like a whiny brat.

It is very possible that the issues within the family and broken relationships that resulted from the prodigal's departure were still present when he returned. It is also very possible that broken relationships, especially sibling relationships, upon your prodigal's departure would still be alive and active upon their return. You'll need to do all you can to help repair the brokenness in your family. You may need additional help. Sometimes, seeking the advice and counsel of a professional is consequential. The broken relationships will need to be mended, and every family member will need to take responsibility for rebuilding their lives. It can be done, but only with the help of the Holy Spirit and only if the family members truly want restoration with one another. There is always hope for reconciliation.

There are many causes for broken sibling relationships, and chief among them is sibling rivalry or jealousy. It seems that siblings are often vying for love, attention, and even acceptance from their parents either because the child has misinterpreted love from a very young age or parents unintentionally pit one child against the other, fostering competition between siblings. Whatever the reason, or the cause, there may be brokenness that results.

I have often spoken with parents who do not understand why their children go in opposite directions when they "have raised them exactly the same." That is the answer to the query. All children are different, with different personalities, different skill sets, and different needs.

Proverbs 22:6 (AMP) says, "Train up a child in the way he should go [teaching him to seek God's wisdom and will for his abilities and talents], Even when he is old he will not depart from it."

Parents should train a child based on their abilities and skill set, not based on what was right for their sibling. When parents try to raise their children exactly the same without taking their differences into consideration, one child will feel frustrated and insecure. It will also create competition between siblings—to be better or, at the very least, just as good. Is that what happened between the prodigal and his older brother? It is also possible that the prodigal knew his older brother would inherit most of his father's estate. So, why try to excel in his own life? Maybe he felt hopeless to compete. It is also possible that the parenting was exemplary—with no rivalry—and the prodigal simply chose to follow the path of sinfulness.

Still, the older brother's reaction seems extreme. He knew his father had prayed and waited for his brother's return. He had probably heard the prayers and maybe seen the tears of his father as he prayed and waited for the return of the prodigal. He knew the anguish the father had experienced. Now the prodigal was home, rescued, redeemed, and the older brother could not rejoice with his father. His father might have been willing to forgive, but he was not. He could not share in the happiness his father felt. He continued to hold his brother's sin against him. He did not have the same heart as his father. He resented his father's joy. So, he refused to share in his father's joy and participate in the celebration, which begs the question: how well did he really know and love his father? Did he share in wanting what his father wanted, and did his heart break for what broke his father's heart? Nothing should have brought him more joy than knowing that a lost soul, his own brother, had come home.

During the time the prodigal had been gone, the older brother had been working and improving his father's holdings. He had worked very hard, sun up until sundown. During the long days in the hot sun and the long days in the cold, windy weather, he continued to work... probably for years. I think it is interesting to note in verse 29 that the older brother says that he has been "slaving" for his father. Some translations use the word "serving." The older brother had resentment. He felt he had been forced to work for his father and obey him. In his mind, he was his father's property, and his father controlled him. He likely worked extremely hard, but it is doubtful that the father realized the depth of his older son's resentment toward his job. His father had already proved to be a generous man, so had he realized the extent of his oldest son's resentment, he probably would have given him more than a goat to roast with his friends. The resentment continued to build in the older brother until the prodigal brother came home, and it boiled over into hurtful words that could not be retracted.

Have you ever watched others do nothing while you work? Maybe you were on a job, and someone slipped away to take a short break, but the short break turned into a long one. You alone were tidying up after a meal while others sat around and talked, doing nothing to help. You were working an event after church, picking up debris, but no one else was interested in getting the job finished. You tried to explain what needed to be accomplished, and the person told you it wasn't in their portfolio.

While we may be doing the right thing, resentment may creep into our spirits. It begins with a little thing, and before we know it, a huge seed has taken root. A tree sprouts, and the fruit of resentment harvests as we tally up all the good we have done when no one took notice. Our motives come into question: are we serving so someone will notice or so that we can please our heavenly Father? If you are serving only for recognition, as it seems the prodigal's brother did, your motives are wrong, and your reward is temporary. As the older brother worked (served and slaved), the prodigal partied, spent money on prostitutes, and used up all he had been given.

Just as the prodigal had listened to the voice of the enemy of his soul telling him that he deserved to have a good time, the older brother had probably begun to listen to that same voice telling him that he was a hard worker, deserving of much more than he was getting. He had done all that was asked of him, everything his father desired. Why couldn't he have time to party? He was never even offered a goat to roast with his friends. He deserved something, some recognition for all his hard work. He was much better than his prodigal brother. Self-righteousness crept into the heart of the older brother until he was unwilling to offer forgiveness when his brother came home. He became the judge and jury against his brother, feeling that the life the prodigal had lived was unforgivable.

Have you ever been there? Have you ever thought the sin of someone else was so grievous that you could not understand how they could be forgiven or how they could do such a horrible thing? May God forgive us all if we become the prodigal's older brother, unwilling to offer forgiveness when our own sin is just as great and just as grievous to our heavenly Father. I believe the prodigal's father recognized that his heir, his older son, was in spiritual danger by harboring unforgiveness. As are we.

Another thing that is very important to note in this passage is that the brother referred to the prodigal as his father's son. He had already let go of the relationship and had no interest in restoration. I can speculate that he denied his brother's existence when people in his village asked about him. He may have said that his father had another son, but he had no brother.

I recently purchased a workbook to log important information concerning the end of life. It had places for bank account numbers, charge card numbers, social media accounts, passwords, pet information, and doctors' offices, but there were a massive number of pages that were devoted to "My Apologies." For some unknown reason, the creator of this workbook thought it was important to include pages for people to write letters of apology to those they had wronged. However, it was only after their death that those letters would be delivered. It seemed to me that if a person knew they needed to write a letter of apology, it should be written and delivered before death, so forgiveness and restoration could begin. That is what pleases our heavenly Father. We are to seek forgiveness for our sin, ask forgiveness of those we have wronged, and forgive those who have wronged us. We shouldn't wait until we are dead and gone, relying on someone else to pass along a letter. I would hate to go into eternity, stand before God, and explain to Him that I left a letter for that person I refused to forgive in life but was willing to forgive in death. I don't want to hear, "Too late." That's a chance I'm unwilling to take.

The book of Matthew has much to say about forgiveness. Matthew 6:14 says, "For if you forgive other people when they sin against you, your heavenly Father will also forgive you." He doesn't stop there:

Then Peter came to Jesus and asked, "Lord, how many times shall I forgive my brother or sister who sins against me? Up to seven times?" Jesus answered, "I tell you, not seven times, but seventy-seven times." —Matthew 18:21-22

And let's not forget about Paul's letter to the Ephesians: "Be kind and compassionate to one another, forgiving each other, just as in Christ God forgave you" (Ephesians 4:32).

How many times have we seen unforgiveness in our own society? Family members become angry with one another and refuse to speak, and years pass by without any efforts towards resolution or restoration. As time passes, many will deny the blood relationship exists. Families are irrevocably broken, and eternal lives are affected.

Unforgiveness also happens in churches and Christian circles. People become angry with one another; they may continue to attend the same church, but they avoid or may even snub one another when they come face to face. Years pass, and no one offers apologies or seeks restoration. There may even be a sense of satisfaction when another person is facing a difficulty: "I knew they had it coming." "You reap what you sow." "There is always a harvest." I have heard so many almost express joy when sorrow comes to someone they haven't forgiven. They have developed a sense of self-righteousness—a pharisaical attitude—just like the older brother of the prodigal.

The story of the prodigal is about the father's love, forgiveness, and restoration and God's love for us. God's love for us is unconditional and is not based on our faithfulness. If He only loved us when we were faithful, we would all be unloved! Even when we are unfaithful, God is still faithfully commanding His love toward us as Romans 5:8 declares: "But God demonstrates his own love for us in this: While we were still sinners, Christ died for us."

That's what makes this story of the prodigal so easy to understand. The father was willing to forgive both of his sons. He was willing to forgive one for disrespect, blatant sinfulness, immorality, and unrighteous living. He was willing to forgive the other son for his own unforgiveness, and a judgmental, self-righteous attitude. They were both committing sins of the body and sins of the heart. The rest of the story, the postscript, so to speak, is not outlined in Scripture. As a result, it is up to us to continue the story for our prodigal when he comes home. I am not speaking about adding to Scripture but putting the practical godly principles into practice to rebuild their lives in your home and restore your family relationships. It HAS to be done. Just as we don't normally spend a lot of time on the brother of the prodigal, we don't spend a lot of time discussing how the prodigal integrated back into his father's home or what it was like to live in his father's home again.

While the Prodigal Is Gone

While the prodigal is gone, make every effort to *not* center your life around their absence, especially if you still have other children at home. You need to continue to live, vacation, and celebrate. Do not spend all your time visibly sorrowing while the prodigal is away. Satan would love to take away your moments of joy and create resentment in the children who are left at home. Your life cannot revolve around the missing, wayward child. If you continue life praying and longing for the prodigal to return rather than establish a holding pattern of despair, you'll save your other children from suffering for the decisions of the prodigal.

Just because a prodigal has chosen to separate from the family does not mean the other family members must lose.

Include the children left at home in prayers for the prodigal. Be assured that they pray for their salvation and their return to the family. Celebrate the wins of your children, their birthdays, athletic games, and the things they hold dear. Just because a prodigal has chosen to separate from the family does not mean the other family members must lose.

Finally, while the prodigal is gone, do your part to prepare for their return. Prepare your heart with love, forgiveness, and acceptance. Anticipate your reactions and deal with them before you have them! Ask yourself the question, "How will I feel if_____?" Prepare your family to do the same. Prepare your home to receive the prodigal and to make a place for their eventual return. Keep a room ready. Keep their clothes washed, folded, and cleaned for them to use when they come home. Be ready to make room for the prodigal both in your home and in your family when they return.

Anticipate their return because they ARE coming home. Don't grow weary. Find your strength in the Lord. You can look to Isaiah 40:28-31 for comfort:

Do you not know?
Have you not heard?
The LORD is the everlasting God,
the Creator of the ends of the earth.
He will not grow tired or weary,
and his understanding no one can fathom.
He gives strength to the weary
and increases the power of the weak.
Even youths grow tired and weary,
and young men stumble and fall;
but those who hope in the LORD
will renew their strength.
They will soar on wings like eagles;
they will run and not grow weary,
they will walk and not be faint.

When the Prodigal Returns

Taking cues from the prodigal's brother's reaction, parents need to know and understand that not everyone will be glad the prodigal has returned. Not everyone will celebrate. Parents have been waiting, praying, and anticipating their return, but some have doubted that it would happen. Some may have expected it but wonder how long they will be home before they return to their prodigal lifestyle.

You may need to ask yourself how much time and effort you are willing to give when your prodigal returns. You have already prayed, fasted, wept, and worried over their absence. Just because your prodigal has returned home does not mean that everything will be peaceful and happy. The battle is not over. There will be struggles.

There may be conflict. In fact, you should probably count on it. Remember, the prodigal may bring home new ideas, new ways of thinking and doing things. Yes, repentance has happened, but sanctification is a process. The prodigal will need to work through some things. Your prodigal may try to test your boundaries, but family rules must still be followed and adhered to. Your other children may remember areas of previous conflict and may be less forgiving than you. They will also remember the pain the prodigal caused the family. They may not have the forgiving heart of a parent so it may be harder for them to let go of the pain and heartache the deeds and absence of the prodigal caused. Allow them to process but encourage forgiveness.

Try to find neutral ground. Integrating the prodigal back into the family will take time and deliberate endurance. Your family issues will not be immediately settled. Some will be resolved simply because of the act of repentance. Others may resurface over time. Family members may bring some of these issues up from time to time. Although an entirely clean slate would be miraculous, it may not happen. If it doesn't, find a place you can compromise and agree. You may need to agree to disagree at times, but remember that as the parent, some things are nonnegotiable under your roof. You decide what those things are.

As you are integrating your prodigal back into the life of your family, finding neutral ground, and continuing to pray and believe God for complete restoration, don't give up. Ephesians 6:12-13 admonishes us to remember the battle is not a flesh-and-blood battle, but a spiritual battle. You are not fighting family members who have no faith in the repentance of the prodigal. You are not fighting the doubters or those who have unforgiveness in their hearts. You are fighting the enemy who wants to continue the destruction of your home and your prodigal. The battle is not over.

> *For our struggle is not against flesh and blood, but against the rulers, against the authorities, against the powers of this dark world and against the spiritual forces of evil in the heavenly realms. Therefore put on the full armor of God, so that when the day of evil comes, you may be able to stand your ground, and after you have done everything, to stand. —Ephesians 6:12-13*

Just stand. Don't waver. You have come this far—it is not the time to quit.

As the Prodigal Grows and Changes

I have mentioned this before, but it bears repeating: don't let go of the dream. As long as you keep the dream alive and keep dreaming, the dream will stay alive. God has given you promises for your children. You have prayed them home, but the battle is not over. There is still a battle for their soul. There are things in their lives that may require extra help, and they may need discipleship.

Give them all the tools they need to succeed again in their Christian life. Remind them of the promises of God for their lives and that God has His hand on them. Don't let go.

Show them how to rebuild your trust. Only you will know how to do that. Just because they are home does not mean that you "give them a new inheritance." Yes, you have forgiven them. Yes, they are reconciled into relationship with the family, but that does not mean that you take away the inheritance from your other children and give it to the prodigal. There is a cost to sinfulness as there is a reward to faithfulness.

There may be things your prodigal needs to finish. Help them do so. One of our prodigals returned to ministry school and finished what God had called her to do. One went into an intense discipleship training program that helped deepen her relationship with Jesus. The important thing that you need to decide is what is needed to help them finish and finish well.

Help them to be restored and do it with the kindness and gentleness of the Holy Spirit, as Galatians 6:1 says: "Brothers and sisters, if someone is caught in a sin, you who live by the Spirit should restore that person gently. But watch yourselves, or you also may be tempted."

The pathways of a prodigal are difficult for everyone involved: parents, siblings, grandparents, aunts, uncles, extended family members, and various loved ones. Be assured that just as it takes many people to raise a child, it takes many to pray a prodigal home. Once we had the spiritual and prayer support of significant family members and loved ones in our lives, our prodigal came home. We never let go of the dream or the promises that God had given to us. In addition, the destiny of God began to be fulfilled in her life. Yes, there were moments of pain that had to be navigated through for all of us, but the joy of having her home and again serving the Lord far outweighed the memories of her pathway as a prodigal. May God grant you and your family that same answer to prayer.

It gave me great joy when some believers came and testified about your faithfulness to the truth, telling how you continue to walk in it.—3 John 3:3-4

Parent's Prayer

Heavenly Father, thank You for hearing my prayers and for bringing me to a place of believing that my prodigal will return home and to Your kingdom. Now I ask You to help prepare me for when it happens. Help me to know how to forgive and help others in my family forgive the pain and heartache our prodigal may have caused. Help us restore the broken relationships and guard against the ever-encroaching spirit of self-righteousness. Help us learn how to resolve conflict and trust You in the process of doing so. Forgive me, Lord, for my many failures, and help me to help others who may also be suffering the pain of a prodigal. Help me to never give up and never lose hope. Help me to know that You will finish the good work that You have started. In Jesus's name. Amen.

Pathways of a Prodigal Notes

From "The Pathways of a Prodigal" sermon, Parts 1 and 2, posted on the Randy Valimont YouTube channel.

Luke 15:11-24

Introduction
Brokenness creates capacity. That capacity should be filled with God's presence and anointing.

Pathways of a Prodigal
A. The Prodigal's_____(verse 12).

    The_____always begins with_____desires.

    The_____ always goes to a _____ _____.

    The _____ always produces _____ (verse 13).

    The _____ will always _____ to _____ and _____.

    The _____ leads to a _____-_____ process.

138 Pathways *of a* Prodigal

The initial decisions are _____ decisions.

_____ decisions can lead the prodigal to the _____ of _____.

The prodigal made a _____ based on _____.

The journey leads to _____, which consists of four things. (verses 18-19).

A _____ of _____ against _____ and _____.

A _____ of his _____.

A _____ to be a _____ servant.

The _____ journey _____.

B. The _____ _____ and _____ (verse 12).

   1. The Father's _____.

   2. The Father's _____.

      a. He let the _____ develop.
       1. Calling the prodigal home too soon will _____ them to their actions.

2. He didn't go _____.
   3. He was willing to _____ and _____.

  b. He provided _____ _____ while the prodigal was in the _____ country.

  c. He was _____ to _____ (verse 20).
   1. _____ in the _____ caused him to stand and _____.
   2. _____ moved him to _____.
   3. He made it _____ to _____.

3. The Father's _____ (verses 20-24).

  a. The _____ to _____.

  b. The _____ to _____
   1. The ring was a _____ of _____.
   2. The shoes were to distinguish he wasn't a _____.

  c. The _____ to _____ (verse 23).
   1. _____ always makes a _____.
   2. _____ always _____ _____.
   3. _____ always _____ _____ and _____ _____.

Conclusion
The pathways of a prodigal are always hard and difficult for everyone _____.

Printed in the USA
CPSIA information can be obtained
at www.ICGtesting.com
JSHW012010250624
65228JS00003B/5

9 781959 095705